Three Crossbows and a Lion Rampant

A HISTORY OF THE HURRELLS OF CAMBRIDGESHIRE

JOHN WALSH AND LESLEY KERR BONE

MEMOIRS

Cirencester

Published by Memoirs

Memoirs Books

25 Market Place, Cirencester, Gloucestershire, GL7 2NX
info@memoirsbooks.co.uk, www.memoirsbooks.co.uk

Copyright © John Walsh and Lesley Bone 2010
First published in England, October 2011
Design and layout by Martin Davis
Book jacket design Ray Lipscombe

ISBN 978-1-908223-32-6

This book is sold subject to the condition that it shall not, by way of trade or otherwise, be lent, resold, hired out, or otherwise circulated without the publisher's prior consent in any form of binding or cover other than that in which it is published and without a similar condition including this condition being imposed on the subsequent publisher. The moral right of the authors has been asserted in accordance with the Copyright, Designs And Patents Act 1988.

NOTICE TO READERS

While great care has been taken to ensure that the information in this publication is accurate, neither John Walsh nor Lesley Bone accept responsibility for any error or omission that may have occurred. It is sold, therefore, on the condition that neither the Compiler nor Editors can be held legally responsible for the consequences of any error or omission there may be.

We welcome comments, suggestions and feedback from readers and users of this book which could help with any possible future editions.

To the memory of
William Hurrell and Elizabeth Head

This book is dedicated to all their living descendants

Major William Hurrell, eldest son of William Hurrell and Elizabeth Head, and husband of Florence (née Dearsley).

Contents

Preface — vii
Acknowledgements — x
Chapter 1   Introduction — 1
Chapter 2   Sible Hedingham, Essex — 7
Chapter 3   Bourn, Sawston and Harston, Cambridgeshire — 15
Chapter 4   Newton, Cambridgeshire — 21
Chapter 5   Back to Harston — 27
Chapter 6   Foxton, Cambridgeshire — 31
Chapter 7   Foxton, the next Generation — 37
Chapter 8   Arkesden, Essex — 53
Chapter 9   The Chancery Case – Arkesden to London — 65
Chapter 10 London – Camden Town — 81
Chapter 11 London – Wandsworth — 93
Appendix 1 Sible Hedingham Hurrells: an unfinished story — 109
Appendix 2 Lucy Gordon – Family Background — 117
Appendix 3 Some other descendants of Allen Hurrell and Lucy Gordon — 125
Appendix 4 Inventory of Elizabeth Hurrell (1671) — 136
Appendix 5 Will of Allen Hurrell (1698) — 138
Appendix 6 Inventory of Allen Hurrell (1700) — 140
Appendix 7 Wills Referred to in this History — 142
Appendix 8 Census Records Referred to in this History — 144
Appendix 9 Documents in Relation to the Case in Chancery of Toplis v Hurrell — 147
Bibliography — 151
Index of Places — 153
Index of People — 156

Illustrations

Photographs

5 Mortimer Lane, Thomas Hurrell's house in Foxton in the early 1600s	12
Allen Hurrell's will drawn up 3 February 1698	23
Inventory of Allen Hurrell's Estate, 1700	24
St. Nicholas' Church, Elmdon Essex	28
Elmdon Church, floor plaques of William Hopkins and his wife, Anna	28
Jane Mortimer (née Hurrell)	32
John H Mortimer, self-portrait	33
Foxton Bury	38
The Hurrell coat of arms	39
Altar and Chancel of Foxton Church	41
Foxton Church in 2011	42
William Hurrell: burial plaque in the Chancel at Foxton Church	42
Foxton House in 2007	46
The Malting House, Foxton	49
The Maltings, Foxton in 1910	50
Hurrell floor plaques in the chancel of Foxton Church	51
Grave of Rebecca Hurrell (née Pottrell)	53
Hobs Aerie farmhouse	54
1821 map of Arkesden and surrounding farms	56
Arkesden Parish Church and the Hurrell family altar tomb	60
Views of modern Arkesden	61
St. Mary the Virgin Church, Arkesden and Little Beckett's Farm	62
Geoffrey Taylor Hurrell and Geoffrey Dearsley Hurrell in Harston in 1979	77
In Memoriam The Hurrell Cranmer Epiphany Trust Fund	79
October 25th 1867 – Baptisms of William, Elizabeth and Mary Hurrell	84
February 1st 1868 – Marriage of William Hurrell and Elizabeth Head	85
February 6th 1870 – Baptism of Henry A. C. Hurrell	85
North London Collegiate School building after closure in 1897 and conversion into a furniture factory	87
Maintaining good order!	88
The unveiling of the statue of Richard Cobden MP in 1868 outside the North London Collegiate School in Camden	88
Undated photograph of boys at London School, possibly at Highgate Rd, St. Pancras	89
William Hurrell of Wandsworth	92
The George and Dragon in the late 1890s	94
Mary (Pollie) Hurrell	95
Major William Hurrell and his wife, Florence (née Dearsley)	98

Florence Hurrell (née Dearsley)	99
The Horseshoe Hotel in Gwelo (two views)	100
Henry A.C. Hurrell	101
Elizabeth Hurrell (née Head)	101
Henry A.C Hurrell and Edith Stone — Wedding photograph	102
Wandsworth Cemetery inscription: E. Hurrell (née Head) and Henry A.C. Hurrell	103
Henry A.C Hurrell and others	104
The Dearsley family group	104
"In Loving Remembrance Henry Allen Conelly Hurrell"	105
Edith Hurrell (née Stone) and Molly in 1903	106
The Field family in 1916	107
The baptism of Moses Hurrell, as in the Sible Hedingham parish register	112
Maria Canning	121
Joseph Cranmer Gordon: death certificate	123
Quendon Church and plaques	124
Certificate of the marriage of William Bailey Hurrell and Agnes Regan	127
A Certificate of Discharge in the name of W. B. Hurrell	127
Elizabeth McGill (née Hurrell) and grand-daughter, Sandra	128
The plaque marking the recasting of the tenor bell at Arkesden	128
Arkesden churchyard: Grave of Allen Hurrell, his wife Mary	129
The stone altar in St. Mary's Church, Brighton, in memory of Ethel A. W. Cranmer	130
The grave of Fanny and Ethel Cranmer	131
Family vaults of the families of A. K. George and his son, Duncan	133
Florence Halcrow (née Byles) with members of her family	134
John Charles Bayles and Ethel Annie (née Dunn)	134
Grave of Elizabeth Ann Hurrell and William Nicholls Dunn	135

Charts

The Hurrell Family	Facing page 1
Hurrell surname distribution 1880-1900	2
Children of George Hurrell and Agnes Hunwick/Ann	6
Children and grandchildren of Allin Hurrell and Elizabeth Thurgood	14
Children of Allen Hurrell, Jane Greenhill and Anne (unknown)	20
Children of Allen Hurrell and Anna Webb	26
Children of William Hurrell and Elizabeth Hurrell	30
Children of William Hurrell and Ann Stacey	36
Children of Allen Hurrell and Lucy Gordon	52
Children of William Hurrell and Elizabeth Head	80
Children and Grandchildren of Henry Cranmer and Margaret	119
Children of Joseph Cranmer Gordon and Mary Ann	123
Children of Allen Hurrell and Mary Bailey	126
Children and grandchildren of Maria Hurrell and Augustin King George	132

Preface

Over the years many people have been engaged in researching this branch of the Hurrell family tree. One person who was active from early on and has continued to the present is Angela Hurrell, wife of Dale, a descendant of Major William Hurrell who died in 1937. In 1967 Joan Mary Woodham Hurrell, a fifth-generation descendant of William Stacey Hurrell of Foxton, Cambridgeshire, wrote to Angela giving her a clue that William Stacey had a younger brother Allen, who lived at Arkesden in Essex and was probably her (Angela's) side of the family. Joan alluded to the Hurrell box tombs in the churchyard at Arkesden and gave the first indication that the family may have come from Sible Hedingham in Essex. Angela made the first attempt to find the registration of the birth of Major William Hurrell, at that time thought to have been born in Arkesden, Essex; she also enquired after his school, North Collegiate, then thought to have been in Cambridge. On both counts she drew a blank. Also, she amassed a number of early family photographs and memorabilia, some of which have been incorporated into this book.

In 1970, Angela was joined by Philippa Bone and Ann Kritzinger, daughters of Phyllis, herself a daughter of the Major. They were the first to make contact with the Hurrells on the Harston side of the family. They were surprised to find that the Harston Hurrells knew little of the Major's branch of the family, although later, in 1975, Mary (Maria) Hurrell of Park House, Harston, did provide some information which helped to fill in a few gaps. Phyllis, also, had accumulated much on the Hurrells including notes and jottings, photographs of her parents and their families, letters such as the letter from her father quoted in Chapter 1 and memorabilia such as her father's gold fob watch with engraved lion-rampant crest shown on the cover.

In 1975, by which time Phyllis had moved to England and joined the search, contact was made with John Richard Hurrell of Hartley, near Dartford in Kent, who was researching his own family tree. John explained that the Hurrells of Sible Hedingham had split into three groups or branches (information he had earlier obtained from the Swann Hurrell Manuscript), the 'Youngest' branch settling in Foxton, Harston and Newton, Cambs, c1590, the 'North Essex' branch settling in Bulmer, Brundon Hall, Maplestead, c1590 and the 'Eldest' branch settling in Boreham, Malden Heybridge, Essex, c1700. He belonged to the North Essex branch.

Over the next two or three years, in correspondence with Phyllis, Ann and Angela, John Hurrell provided much information about the Hurrell coat of arms and parts of the Hurrell family tree, as well as details from various parish registers. There were gaps and some inaccuracies but nevertheless there was much that proved to be useful. In December 1975, John came up with some discoveries that were particularly significant. Although quite a lot was known of the Major's father's ancestors, nothing was known about his mother. John unearthed the birth register entries of the Major's brothers, Henry Allen C. and Henry Ernest, where it was recorded that the mother was Elizabeth Head and the father was a brewer by occupation. He also produced the index of death of the Major's father in 1878 in Wandsworth, London, who was by then a Licensed Victualler. These facts turned out to be very useful later.

Another important source of information at this time was Rowland Parker's book *The Common Stream* published in 1975 which anchored the Hurrells in Foxton and provided much background detail of the lives of 18th and 19th century village people.

In February 1976 John Hurrell sent Phyllis a copy of the Swann Hurrell Manuscript written about 1892 with John's own notes as a preface. John noted that the original manuscript was in the possession of John Sopwith Hurrell, then late of North Shields, Newcastle. His notes elaborate on the family arms and mottoes and his own family tree. As noted in Chapter 2 of this book, the Manuscript suggests a link with Sible Hedingham without establishing the connection. Then there are brief notes on the Foxton Hurrells down to Swann's generation all of which were useful and which John elaborated further in May 1976. Although fragmentary, the Manuscript is interesting as one of the first attempts to delve into the history of this branch of the Hurrell family.

When Phyllis left England in 1978 correspondence ceased and work on the Hurrells lapsed. Nobody had the time or means to do more than scratch the surface until Lesley Kerr Bone, daughter of Philippa, took it upon herself to put the history together in 1997. She had all the necessary attributes to do the work:

computer skills, investigative ability, persistence and a rational mind. Where possible, all relationships were supported by records, for example birth, death and marriage registrations, parish records of baptisms, deaths and marriages, census records, directories, newspaper notices, wills and more. Lesley built up a database using the software *Family Tree Maker*. Only a part of the database has been used in the writing of this book. One significant piece of information she obtained was by finding the records of the Chancery case affecting the Hurrells of Arkesden (which came to light by way of legal notices in an 1856 edition of *The Times* of London). More clever sleuthing was executed in bringing to light the family of Elizabeth Head and her eventual marriage to the Major's father. As time went on, more and more genealogical information was put online which made Lesley's task less onerous but no less exacting.

When Martin and Elizabeth (Beth) Davis contacted Lesley a few years ago, they filled in one of the last pieces of the puzzle, that is what had become of the descendants of the Major's brother Henry Allen Conolly Hurrell. Beth and her sister, Susan Rawlins are the daughters of Henry's only daughter Molly. Martin and Beth produced many photographs and memorabilia not seen before, which added to the understanding of the George and Dragon pub scene and the Wandsworth period. With single-mindedness, Martin pursued the link with the Hurrells in Sible Hedingham, and his research has formed the basis of Chapter 2 and Appendix 1. Although there are a few missing records, there is now strong evidence that the Hurrells described in this book are the descendants of George Hurrell of Sible Hedingham. George's son, Allyn (or Allin) Hurrell, moved away from Sible Hedingham to Sawston and then to Bourn, both in Cambridgeshire, and is undoubtedly the ancestor we have been looking for. Martin has also contributed by setting up the book on his computer, designing the format, and using his expertise both to date early family photos and to transcribe old wills.

As already stated, neither all the information in Lesley's database nor all the photos could be incorporated in the book. We had to be selective and try to stay as close as possible to the direct male line of descent. It is worth mentioning that this history is an attempt to find the origins of this branch of the Hurrells and it is not meant to be a complete history of the Hurrells in England or Rhodesia, the latter subject being one that Angela and others would be much better qualified to write. In writing this book much useful constructive criticism and suggestions have been made by all parties concerned, including John Walsh's wife, Doreen.

Acknowledgements

Our thanks go to those who have helped in the production of this book. We owe a debt of gratitude to Martin Davis who designed the layout, transcribed many old wills, and researched the Hurrell connection to Sible Hedingham, described in Chapter 2 and Appendix 1.

John's wife, Doreen, gave valuable advice and suggestions when reading the early drafts. She also compiled the author's note on the back cover. Details of family relationships can be confusing, so her critical review from the perspective of the outsider was most helpful.

In following up lines of research, Lesley made contact with many people who provided important information on her behalf. In particular, Michael and Lynne Ball, who made available certificates on the descendants of William Bailey Hurrell in Australia. Our thanks also go to the Halcrow and Bayles families, both descendants of Elizabeth Ann Hurrell, for providing photographs for the book.

Our publisher, Memoirs Publishing, has given us much useful advice in the approach to publishing for which we are grateful.

We also acknowledge the generosity of the following for use of pictures, illustrations and information in this book:-

Allen Hurrell's Will & Inventory from the Cambridgeshire Archives.

The Self Portrait of John H. Mortimer titled 'John Hamilton Mortimer A.R.A. Self-Portrait' from The Royal Academy.

The picture of The Maltings House, Foxton, drawn by Rowland Parker.

The picture of The Maltings, Foxton 1910, from The Cambridgeshire Collection, Cambridge Central Library.

Marriage certificate of William Hurrell and Elizabeth Head courtesy of the City of London, London Metropolitan Archives.

Baptism certificate of William, Elizabeth and Mary Hurrell courtesy of the City of London, London Metropolitan Archives.

Baptism certificate of Henry A. C. Hurrell courtesy of the City of London, London Metropolitan Archives

Marriage certificate of William Bailey Hurrell and Agnes Regan are reproduced with the permission of the NSW Registry of Births Deaths & Marriages for and on behalf of the Crown in and for the State of New South Wales and is subject to Crown copyright.

Baptism certificate of Moses Hurrell reproduced by courtesy of Essex Record Office.

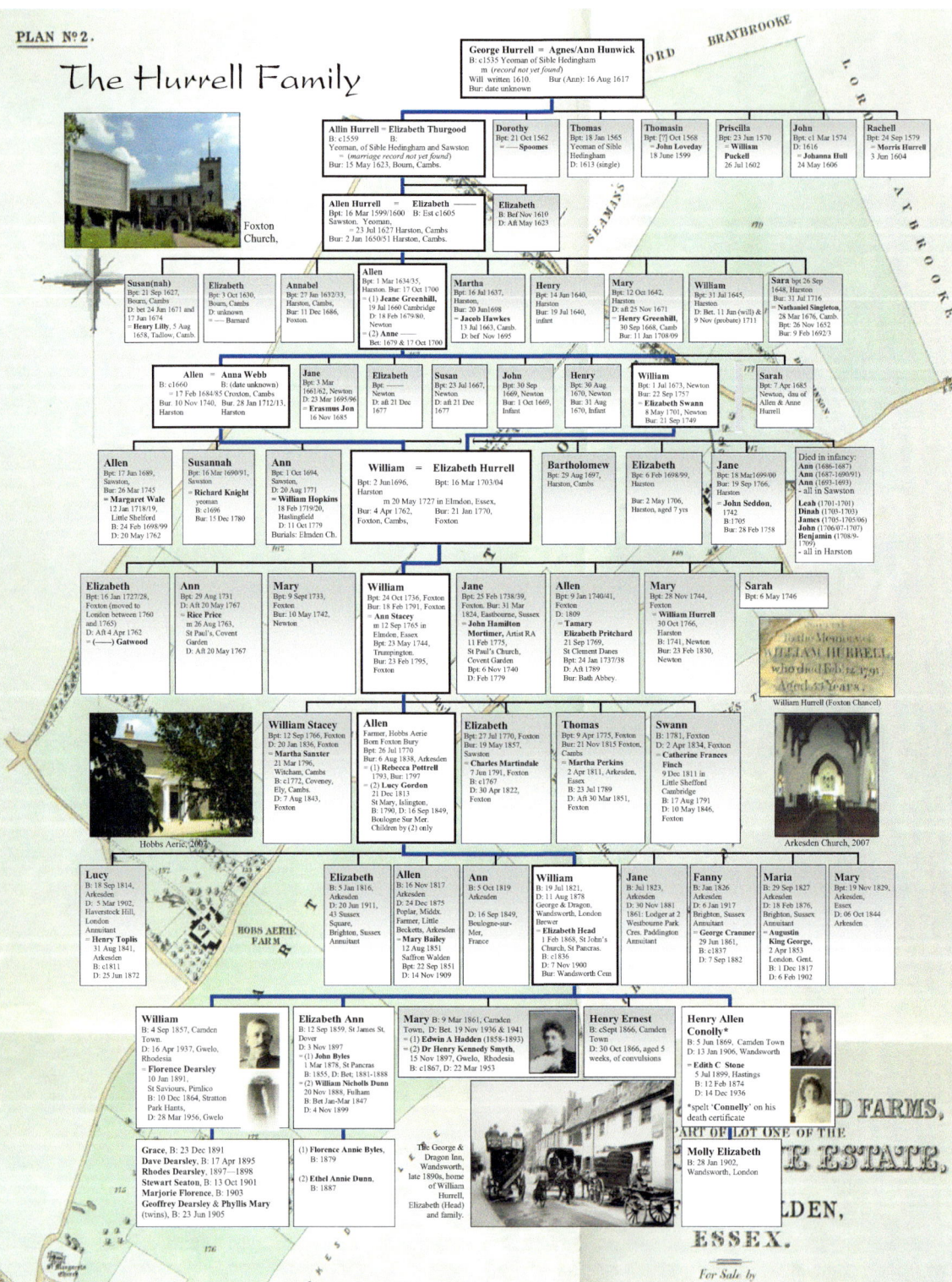

Chapter 1

Introduction

The *Dictionary of Surnames* by Patrick Hanks and Flavia Hodges (Oxford 1988) has this to say about the name 'Hurrell':

'English (Norman) derivative of the diminutive of the French *Huré*, a nickname for someone with an untidy head of shaggy hair, from the past participle of the Old French *hurer* to bristle, ruffle, stand on end.
Variations: Hurran, Hurren
Dims: Hurd, Hureau, Hurot, Huron, Hurrell.'

Very likely the name came to England with the Normans. Towards the end of the 19th century the name was concentrated in the South East of England spreading along the south to Devon and Cornwall and north through the Midlands to Yorkshire, with a local concentration around London, Middlesex and Essex (see map on the next page from The Genealogist UK website). We are now certain that this branch of the Hurrells derives from Sible Hedingham in Essex. The evidence comes from some detailed wills from the early 1600s, but without the full corroborating evidence of all the relevant births and marriages. However, an unbroken line begins in the mid-1500s in Sible Hedingham which, in the early 1600s, moves to Cambridgeshire, around the villages of Sawston, Bourn, Harston, Foxton and Newton.

Chapter 1

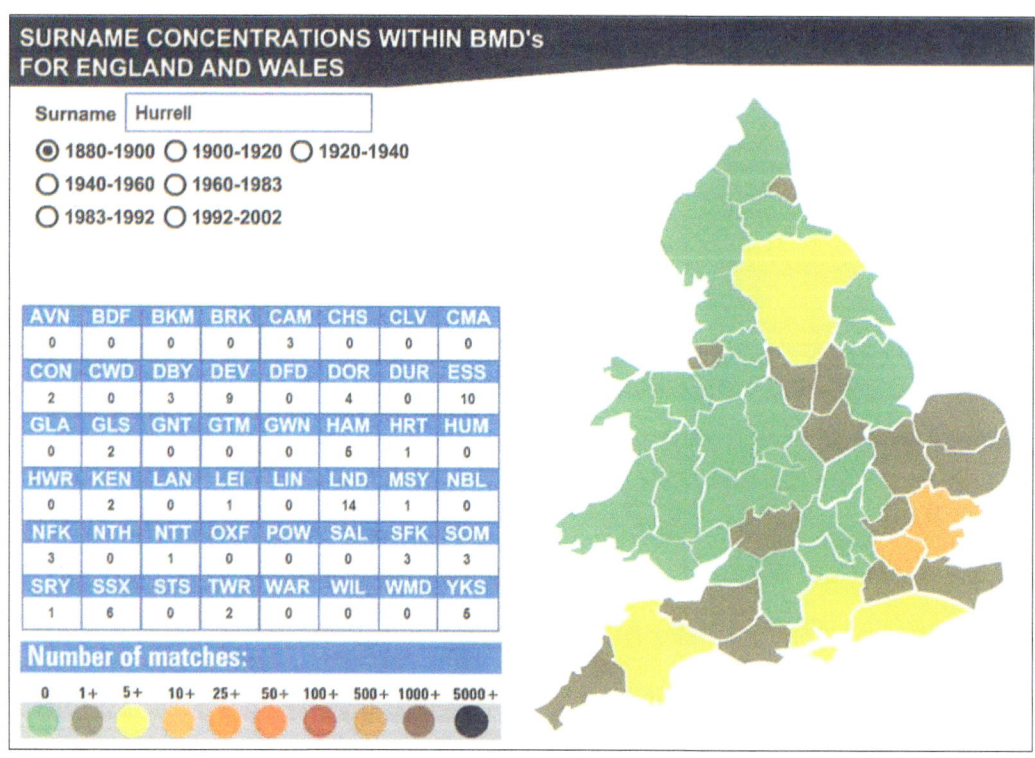

CAM: Cambridgeshire
CON: Cornwall
DBY: Derbyshire
DEV: Devon
DOR: Dorset
ESS: Essex
GLS: Gloucestershire
HAM: Hampshire
HRT: Hertfordshire
KEN: Kent
LEI: Leicestershire
LND: London & Middlesex
MSY: Merseyside

NFK: Norfolk
NTT: Nottinghamshire
SFK: Suffolk
SOM: Somerset
SRY: Surrey
SSX: Sussex
TWR: Tyne & Wear
YKS: Yorkshire

BMDs: Births, Marriages and Deaths.

Hurrell surname distribution 1880 – 1900.

Introduction

In 1934, a descendant, Major William Hurrell of Gwelo, Rhodesia, as it then was, wrote to his daughter, Phyllis, in India, as she was about to travel to England with her family on leave. This letter was pivotal in tracing his ancestors from the 18th to the 20th century. It is transcribed here in full, retaining the original spellings and punctuation:

16th Feby 1934

P.O. Harston,
Zaloba Siding
S. Rhodesia

My Darling Phyllis

You wrote me some time ago to let you know about our family, and if there were any places you might see when at home -
So I am enclosing some particulars in case you go through Cambridgeshire - your Aunt Pollie and I are the only two of the family alive now, and no doubt in the ordinary course of things we shall be gone in a few years. The Hurrells are an old County family -

Coat of arms: 3 bows and arrows
Crest: Lion rampant with banner and cross
It is what is called a Canting coat of arms - quarrel/Hurrell an arrow.
In the Doomsday Book - a famous shooter - County Cambridgeshire.

My grandfather Allen was born at Foxton Hall, Foxton, Cambs. which was owned by my great grandfather William - we owned a little land in the village still when I was a boy - but my father sold it when the franchise came, as the only reason for keeping it was a vote for Cambridgeshire - and of course with the franchise the landed vote was lost - The Asplins owned Foxton Hall then and invited any of us to visit them, they being in the old home of the Hurrells - Harston Hall - Harston was owned by a cousin - but had also gone into other hands - If you go to Foxton or Harston, you will (see) ancestor's names in the church chancels of these places - Newton Hall - Newton Cambs is still owned by a Hurrell.

When my grandfather was alive we were all a united family - my father spent a lot of time there -When my grandfather died he left William Hurrell of

Chapter 1

Newton, and John Canning - I have forgotten his place - his Executors - and some years afterwards my Father and Uncle thought something was wrong as Canning was giving many more dinner parties, and keeping a lot more hunters, than they thought his income would allow - and they told William of Newton this but he said it was impossible - John Canning was a gentleman, and if such a thing happened - of course he would be liable - well later things were looked into and it was found that Canning had robbed the Estate of £40,000 - and he cleared to France - Then they asked William of Newton to make it good, but he then did not see it - so they went to law. The Estate was put in Chancery, it dragged on for 7 years - by which time the rest of the family had grown up, and the girls wanted their money, so they compromised - William of Newton giving £20,000 - and the lawyers got a lot. There were 9 children and they got £10,000 each - Of course thru' this all the old family friendships ceased, and we never met again. My grandfather's seat was Hobbes Eyrie, Arkesden, Essex, and that was sold too.

Newton Manor belonged to another William Hurrell, who died some years ago - I did not know him.

Maddingley Hall - Maddingley, Cambs - belonged to Henry Hurrell - King Edward when Prince of Wales and up at Cambridge stayed here - his son Col Hurrell I heard sold the place to some baronet. Its quite a show place - Swann Hurrell, called by the family the Iron Duke - lived at Cambridge and when I was spoken about in '96 - wrote to the Cambridge Chronicle, giving them my pedigree, as he had been asked if I belonged to the Cambridgeshire family - he also wrote to my Aunt Lucy telling me to visit him when I came home - he and my father were a great deal together when young men - I regret to say that I did not see him.

William Hurrell of Newton lived to a very old age - must have been in the 90's as Bill Crawford Hurrell of Salisbury showed me a snap he took of him somewhere in the nineties - and he was years older than my father who was born in 1821 and died in 1878 after I had come out to South Africa.

I think that is about enough of our people for the present.

Lots of love to you, Phyllipa, John & Sonny

your affec.

Daddy

Introduction

Mother will give you all the news in her letter.

By the way.

You remember Robertson who married Hilda Stuart - he was a nephew of Mrs Nash of Royston Park, Cambs. I expect she would be the next generation but the one Mrs Nash of Royston was a Miss Hurrell and was engaged to my Father but the family made them break it off as they were considered too poor. I suppose this generation would have told them to go to the devil. Robertson knew the present generation of Hurrells at Newton - he said they were crocked up thro' the war and were not well off - of course that is the case with most of the old families.

The last I heard of the Newton lot - they had the American Ambassador staying with them during the war on a visit.

Thats all for the present!

In this history it soon becomes apparent that there is a William and an Allen in practically every generation with the result that it becomes thoroughly confusing at times to identify which generation is being discussed. Consequently, Major William Hurrell the author of the above letter is usually referred to as 'the Major' and thus he forms a reference point in the history particularly in relation to the 19th century.

As generation succeeds generation there is a general movement from village to village gradually moving further afield over time. Thus, the first known generation is associated with Sible Hedingham in Essex, the second with Bourn in Cambridgeshire, the third with Sawston, the fourth with Harston, the fifth with Newton, the sixth back to Sawston and Harston, the seventh and eighth with Foxton, the ninth with Arkesden in Essex and the tenth with London. Thereafter the spread is much further afield to other parts of England and Africa. This is a generalisation but it helps in following the history. From the 4th to the 10th generation the average number of children per generation was about eight, and although infant and child mortality was not infrequent it will be apparent that it will not be possible to follow the careers of every sibling in detail in every generation.

* * * * *

Children of George Hurrell and Agnes/Ann Hunwick

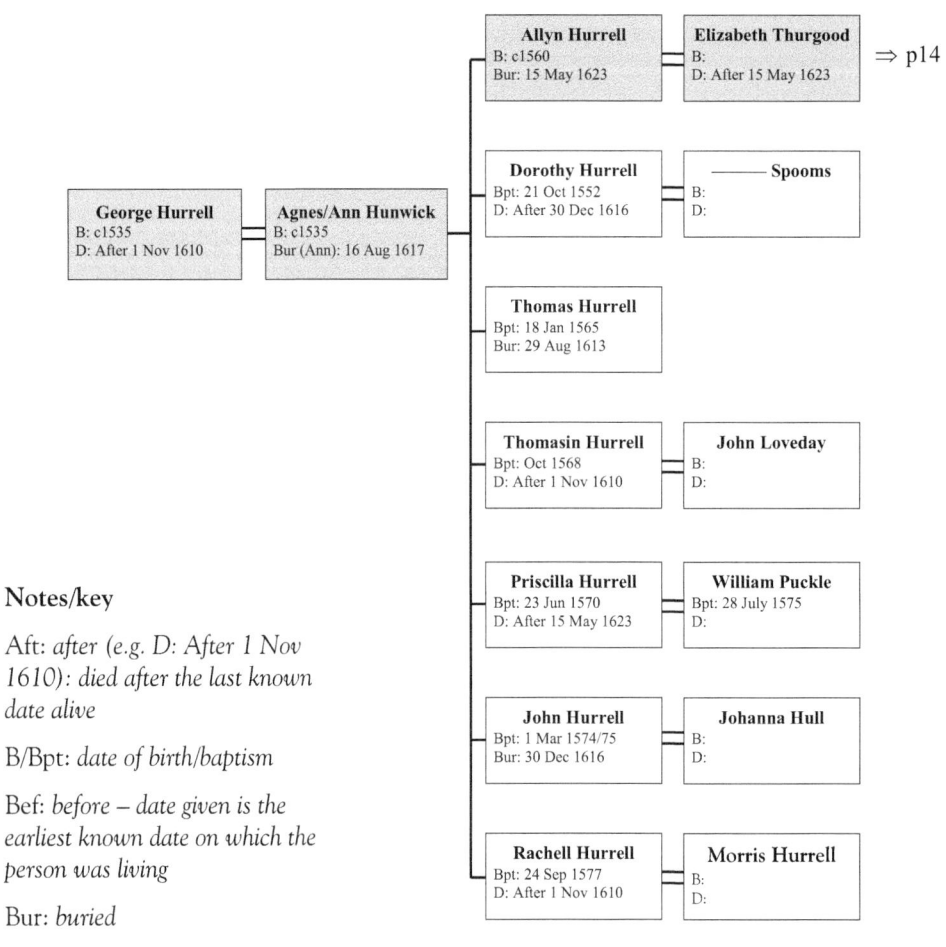

⇒ p14

Notes/key

Aft: *after (e.g. D: After 1 Nov 1610): died after the last known date alive*

B/Bpt: *date of birth/baptism*

Bef: *before – date given is the earliest known date on which the person was living*

Bur: *buried*

D: *died*

c: *(e.g. c1535): about (1535)*

Dates before 1752: *In 1752, Britain changed from the Julian to the Gregorian calendar. The former had become increasingly inaccurate, and the change brought dates in line with those used in much of Europe. The change moved the start of the year back from 25 March to 1 January. A consequence is that, for example, 7 March 1729 as understood at the time, would be 7 March 1730 according to a modern calendar. To avoid ambiguity the date is often written as 7 March 1729/30. This can be confusing to the general reader. In this book dates are in the modern (Gregorian) form, except for those in the charts where the dual system has been retained.*

Chapter 2

Sible Hedingham, Essex

Sible Hedingham is an ancient village with its origins stretching back into the Bronze Age. It lies by the River Colne in the Essex countryside, a few miles north-west of Halstead. Now, the A1017 carries traffic through the village and on to Haverhill, where it joins the A1307 for the last 18 miles to Cambridge. Just south of the city the road passes close to Sawston. Both Sawston and Sible Hedingham are central to the early years of this narrative of the Hurrell family. In the 16th century and earlier, both villages would have been smaller than now, each comprising a mixture of houses and farms loosely surrounding a church.

St Peter's Church in Sible Hedingham stands on a low hill with the older part of the village spread out below. In the 16th century, the village was, perhaps, the home of the greatest concentration of families bearing the name Hurrell in the whole of Essex – between 1540 and 1640 nearly half of all the Essex Hurrell wills originated in this village. Of course, not everyone had enough money or possessions to make a will necessary – so perhaps instead we should say that the village was home to the greatest concentration of successful and, in some cases, wealthy Hurrells.

The earliest known will, written in 1540, is that of Roger Hurrell. He had a wife, Margaret, a son, William and daughters, Margaret and Maud. William is a name that passes down through the Hurrell families within the village and one that keeps reappearing in the Hurrell line throughout this book, well into the reign of Queen Victoria. While it is almost certain that all the Hurrell families living in Sible Hedingham were related to each other in some way, it has not been possible to trace a direct line back to Roger or any other Hurrell family of the mid-1500s – except one. Unfortunately, the early baptisms register, which dates from 1560, does not include the mothers' names. This, and the absence of any marriage records before 1599, makes it almost impossible to establish how many of the Hurrell families, perhaps more than a dozen in the late 1500s, were related to each other.

Most of the Hurrells were yeoman farmers, that is farmers who owned at least some of the land they worked. A few may have described themselves as gentlemen, particularly those living in the larger houses. One, William Hurrell, probably the son of John Hurrell, and grandson of an earlier William, both of Warners, in his will of 1593 left his *...mansion house called Warners...* to his son, also called William (of Lamarsh). There were very few Hurrell families living in the nearby surrounding villages – as is evident in the early parish registers. The Hurrells of Sible Hedingham must have been a close community that preferred, as their numbers grew, to remain in or near the village.

Our story begins in the reign of Henry VIII, with George Hurrell, a successful, possibly wealthy, farmer, who was probably born sometime around 1535. From his will, dated 1610, we know that George was married to Ann, and there were seven children alive when the will was written: Allyn, probably born before the baptisms register started in July 1560, then Dorothy (baptised, 21 Oct 1562), Thomas (18 Jan 1565), Thomasin (Nov 1568 – the day is unclear), Priscilla (23 June 1570), John (1 March 1575) and lastly, Rachell, who was baptised on 24 Sept 1577. All, except Thomas, married. Allyn, John and Thomas refer, in their various wills, to their sister Puckle: Priscilla married William Puckell in 1602. Rachell married Morris Hurrell in 1604.

George made his sons Thomas and John his Executors, and 'brother' (brother-in-law) Francis Hunwick, supervisor of the will. Francis was probably the son of Alane Hunwick, yeoman, of Halstead. In his will (1567), Alane names his son Francis and daughter Agnes Hurrell. He also names George Hurrell as his son-in-law. George may have married twice, first to Agnes Hunwick and later to Ann. There is, however, no burial of Agnes Hurrell in Halstead or Sible Hedingham parish records between the deaths of Alane Hunwick and George Hurrell. It is probable that Agnes, then often pronounced Annis, became shortened to Ann. It is almost certain that Allyn's mother was a Hunwick. In his will of 1623, Allyn names his uncle, Francis Hunwick.

The eldest son, Allyn, was not an Executor of his father's will, and close scrutiny of the document suggests how this might have come about. He was, however, the first named beneficiary in the will *...I give and bequeathe unto Allyn Hurrell my sonne my messuage and tenement wherein I nowe dwell, and all the Free landes meadowe and pasture thereunto belonginge with there appurtenances, To houlde to him and to his heires males begotten or to be begotten ymmediatelye From and after the deceasse of me and my wyfe Ann...* The next word is both cautionary and interesting: *Provided...* It would seem that Allyn and his wife, Elizabeth, should have handed to George some time earlier, a lease document... *which I* [George] *made to the saide Elizabeth of my messuage or Tenement and Orchard and pightle* [a small piece of land] *situate lyinge and being in Sawson* [Sawston], *in the Countie of Cambridge.* Allyn and Elizabeth had to hand over the document within 28 days of George's death. The will continues: *my will and meaning is that my saide sonne Allyn nor his heires nor Assignes shall have any estate right tyttyle* [title] *or demande whatsoever of in or to my saide messuage Tenement or Free landes thereto belonging...* If Allyn does not comply the inheritance passes to George's son, John. There is a further sting – if Allyn does comply and inherits the land and buildings, he is barred from selling any part of it. Should he attempt to do so the land and property immediately passes to John. All this would have been a snub by George to his eldest son; a measure of the possible breakdown in the relationship between them.

Between 1599 and 1611 Allyn is described as a yeoman of Sible Hedingham. Documents in the Essex Archives show that during this period he was involved in leasing land from a local charity, and with an Almshouse property in Aldersford Street. After 1611 such references stop: Allyn is later living in Bourn in Cambridgeshire, where he, aged about 64, wrote his will in 1623, and was buried there a few days later, in the local churchyard.

Chapter 2

In 1599, Allyn and Elizabeth must have been in Sawston, possibly living there in George's house. Their son Allen was born in that year in Sawston. Perhaps their daughter Elizabeth was also born there, although the record of her birth has yet to be found. She is mentioned in George's will, so was already alive in 1610. If Allyn and Elizabeth were based in Sawston between Allen's birth and George's death, Allyn must have spent sufficient time in Sible Hedingham to carry out his charitable obligations there.

It is clear from his will that George had acquired or inherited quite a property portfolio: he may have owned the leases or the properties outright – in Halstead, Sawston as well as Sible Hedingham. One such property in Sible Hedingham had a curious name: Mekitoes or Metitoes, which may have comprised more than one dwelling. George left Mekitoes, which was located at *'Highsted Grene'* within Sible Hedingham, to his son John, and if John were to die without producing any sons – *lawfully begotten*, of course – the house and land would be transferred to Thomas. If Thomas failed to produce a male heir. ownership would transfer to Allen, son of Allyn and Elizabeth. John, it seems, only had three daughters and Thomas died single in 1613, so Allen inherited Mekitoes on John's death in 1616. It is clear that George must have feared that his children would dispose of his property empire, and once again he inserts a conditional clause to prevent such disposal by John. Should he attempt to do so, then Mekitoes would go to the next heir in succession *...without any further delay.*

George's will is both lengthy and detailed, spelling out exactly how each of his seven children was to benefit from its various clauses. Thomas inherited his house called The White Hart in Sawston. This could be the dwelling in Sawston which was the subject of the lease problem involving Allyn and Elizabeth: The White Hart had an orchard and pightle. Once again there is a conditional clause requiring Thomas to have a male heir, or the property will revert to John. Thomas also was bequeathed a croft in Halstead, and if he failed to produce a male heir and *...kepeinge it in sufficient repare...*, the croft would revert to John and his heirs. Morris Hurrell, Rachell's husband, was left *ten pounds of lawfull English mony out of my movables and household stuf*. Should Morris die before the death of Ann, George's wife, the ten pounds was to be paid to William, Morris's son, born March 1605. Thomasin inherited *...my lyttle house wherein Parr...* – (here the corner of the will is missing) – *[to] houlde* *to her and her Assigns for her naturall lyfe...* After Thomasin's death the little house was to pass to Allyn *and his heirs for ever.* Priscilla was not forgotten: *...I give and bequeathe to Priscilla my daughter my lyttle house wherein Whithead dwelled belonging to Mekitoes.* Neither Dorothy nor Rachell inherited property, but the children of all George's daughters were left forty shillings each (about £200 today), to be paid when they each reach the age of twenty-one. Perhaps Dorothy and Rachell's husbands were sufficiently well off: there is no clue in the will. There is one touching detail in George's will: *I give and bequeath unto Elizabeth the daughter of my sonne Allyn Hurrell and to Ann the daughter of my sonne John Hurrell, to each of them a lambe to be delivered to them at their severall ages of one and twenty yeres.* The Sible Hedingham baptism register lists the birth of Ann to John Hurrell, baptised on 1 October 1607. Elizabeth, Allyn's daughter, may well have been born around this time. George may have bequeathed something that he did not own – two unborn lambs! The date and place of George's burial has yet to be discovered.

In the event, George was probably right to insert protective clauses into his will as examination of the wills of John and Thomas shows bequests of lower value than those of their father George. John's nuncupative (oral) will is very hard to decipher, but it does contain a curious line: *Also being asked what shall become of the land he said I have no land...* John does remember his *syster Puckle,* Priscilla, leaving her 20 shillings.

Thomas, likewise refers to his sister Puckle in his will dated 29 August 1613, leaving her children 20 marks, about £13 at the time (equivalent to about £1,300 now), to be equally divided between them. Thomas does however have property in the neighbouring county *...whereas I have laid out money upon a living in Foxon* (Foxton) *in CamBridge sheer.* Rowland Parker, in his book, *The Common Stream,* about the 2,000-year history of Foxton, identifies Thomas Hurrell's house (see the photograph on the next page) as 5 Mortimer Lane. It still stands, much modified over time. The 20 marks bequeathed by Thomas to his sister Priscilla's children, was to come from this house in Foxton. Thomas's will is very brief, only 15 lines in all, and difficult to read. There appears to be no mention of what was to become of 5 Mortimer Lane. As we shall see, Allyn Hurrell's descendants returned later to Foxton, having a significant impact on the life of the village in the 18th century.

Chapter 2

5 Mortimer Lane as it is now, hidden by trees, formerly the Foxton home of Thomas Hurrell, of Sible Hedingham, in the early 1600s.

There is no sign of Allyn, Elizabeth and their two children living in Sible Hedingham, either just before or after George's death. He could not have inherited George's house there until after the death of his mother, Ann, in 1617. That he next appears living in Bourn, a few miles west of Cambridge, may indicate that he failed to meet the conditions in his father's will.

It is worth quoting here in full the oral will left by Allyn's brother John, perhaps just before he died. It creates a vivid image: three witnesses – Robert Browne, Geo(rge) Smith and Morrice Hurrell – attended John as he lay on his death bed, endeavouring to catch his dying wishes, which were duly noted, but stripped of the usual legal jargon. John was buried on 30 December 1616.

> *Memorandum that John Hurrell of Himingham Sible in the countie of Essex did saye these words or the Lyke in effect   I will that Johan my wyfe shall have all that lyvinge which was her owne before I marryed with her with all the stock and croppe thereon   And I will that my children shall have all my moveable goods to be equally divided amongst them all three when they shall accomplish their severall ages of xxi yeares and my wyf to have the rest of the said moveables to bring them up   And also I will that Dorothie Spoomes my kinswoman shall have xx s[1] and my syster Puckle xx s.*

Also the said John Hurrell said I will that my mother shall have some of my corne for that she doth want corne and I have been behoulding to her kindnes then he being asked by one of the standers by how much she should have he made noe answer then the said partie said to him shall she have a seame[2] or half a seame he answered I 1 half a seame.

Also being asked what shall become of your land he said I have no land then said that same partie I to him agayne you have half an acre in the meadow to whom he answered my brother[3] must have it he and I are agreed for that paying for it as it cost me which was xx l[1].

1. xx s: 20 shillings / xx l: 20 pounds (£)
2. Seam/seame: a cartload
3. This must be Allyn, as Thomas died in 1613.

* * *

A little over 250 years later, in 1876, a descendant of Allyn, Swann Hurrell, visited Sible Hedingham. He had read Thomas Wright's book *The History and Topography of Essex*. In volume 2 it is stated that *William Hurle held lands at Havering Attic Bower in 1166*. Swann visited the church in Sible Hedingham and *...by the courtesy of the Rev. (Henry) Warburton, the Rector; I examined and copied the following names and dates.* There follows a list of 12 names taken from the recorded deaths starting with William Hurrell, buried in 1562, the very first name in the register, and ending with Hannah, who died in 1807. He must have had only a short time to look at the documents, perhaps not wishing to take up too much of the Rector's time. He would have had little enough time to become familiar with the old and various styles of writing used. His list only scratches the surface, leaving the majority of Hurrell burials unrecorded. Swann Hurrell, who was born in 1816, had read an old copy of *The Gazeteer & London Daily Advertiser*, dated 22 November 1762: *A few days since died aged 63 at Stoke-juxta-Clare in Suffolk, Miss Sarah Hurrell a maiden gentlewoman, descended from an Ancient Family of that name in Essex for near 700 years; the last 30 years of her life, she had lost the entire use of her limbs, which melancholy condition she supported not only with Resignation but Cheerfulness.*

Without knowing the exact relationships, Swann Hurrell had stumbled across his ancestral line.

* * * * *

Children and grandchildren of Allin Hurrell and Elizabeth Thurgood

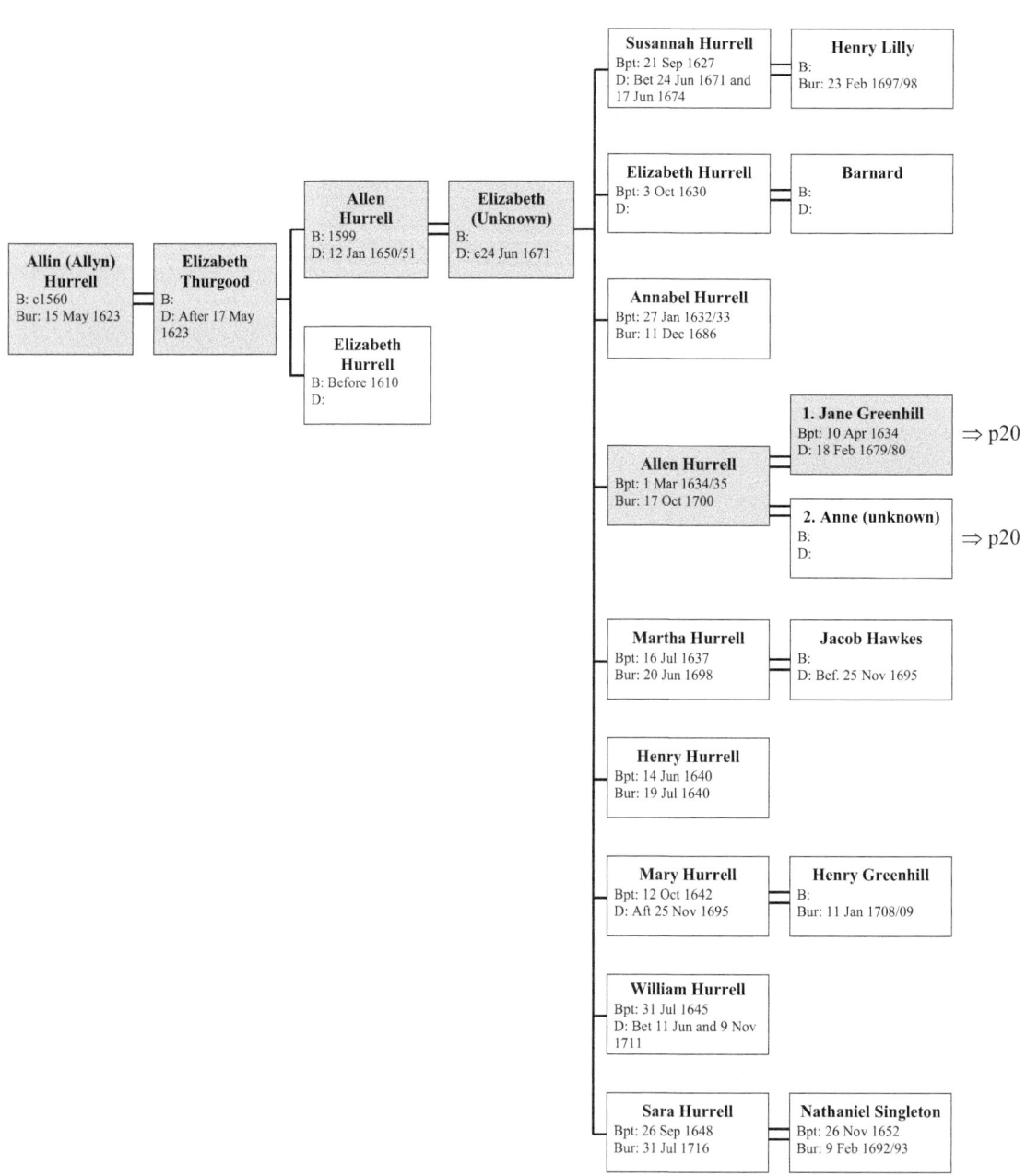

Chapter 3

Bourn, Sawston and Harston, Cambridgeshire

Allin Hurrell, yeoman, settled into farming in Bourn in Cambridgeshire some time after the death of his father, George, in 1610. In 1623, he drew up his will and died a few days later. In his will he adopts the spelling Allin and that will be used in this chapter. His life had encompassed the whole of the first Queen Elizabeth's reign. She had yet to come to the throne when he was born. England was about to enter a period of great resurgence. Allin may have been in his early thirties when the Spanish Armada was defeated in 1588 and in his forties when Shakespeare was at the height of his creativity as a poet and playwright.

Allin's will is dated 15 May 1623 from which we can deduce that he married Elizabeth Thurgood and in which he mentions only his sibling brothers John and Thomas, who had both predeceased him, and a 'sister Puckles' (Priscilla). He left money to the parish church of Sible Himingham (Hedingham) *six shilling eight pence of lawfull money of England*. That may not sound much but

Allin was actually quite well off. He left his wife a house... *(I) give unto Elizabeth my wiffe my house wherein Edward Snellock now dwelleth in for terme of hir naturall liffe shee keepinge it in sufficient repayre duringe the said tyme and comitting no waste theron...* and yearly three loads of wood, a cow and seven pounds a year *duringe hir naturall liffe*. Four years before the will was written the Sible Hedingham parish register records the birth of Robert to Edward and Alice Snellock– the house must have lain within the village. Allin's son, Allen, got the bulk of the inheritance, *all my lands both free and coppye* (copyhold). [Copyhold land, as distinct from freehold land, was land held from a manor. Although copyhold land could be bought, sold or inherited, each transfer of land had to have the approval of the owner of the manor and sometimes there were obligations on the part of the tenant. An official copy of the court roll entry of the transfer was kept by the tenant, hence the term 'copyhold'.] Allin's son also got all the rest of the goods and chattels, implements and household stuff not otherwise given or bequeathed elsewhere. Allin left his daughter, Elizabeth *twentie shillings* and he left something to each of the children of his brothers and sisters. He was buried on 17 May 1623 only two days after he signed his will with his mark. The fact that he signed with his mark in this case does not necessarily mean he was uneducated, he could have been too sick to sign his name.

Allin's son Allin, or Allen, was baptised on 16 March 1600 in Sawston, Cambridgeshire. He also called himself a yeoman and during his life amassed an estate in Harston. He married Elizabeth (her maiden name has not been found) on 23 July 1627 in Harston and they had nine children over the period 1627 to 1648 of whom two died young. Elizabeth gave birth to the first two children in Bourn, Cambridgeshire, but the rest were born in Harston. Three of the children had a later connection with Foxton: Annabel ended her days living in Foxton and Sara married Nathaniel Singleton, a major farmer of his time, in Foxton.

Allen signed his will on 25 December 1650 and was buried on 2 January 1651. Allen's wife Elizabeth also drew up a will which she signed with her mark on 20 June 1671 and was buried on 24 June 1671 in Harston. Both she and Allen drew up their wills when *sicke and weake in body but of sound and perfect memory*.

The designation 'yeoman' gives us an idea of the social status of these Hurrells. They were yeoman farmers, that is they were people who lived on and farmed the land they owned, unlike the landed gentry who usually employed tenant farmers and lived elsewhere. The gentry usually had larger land holdings than the yeomen and were located between the yeomanry and the peerage in social status.

Again we have the connection with Sible Hedingham in Essex. In his will, Allen left his house and tenement, Mekitoes, in Potters Street in Sible Himingham (Hedingham) that he had acquired from his grandfather, George, to his wife until such time as his eldest son, also Allen, attained the age of 24 years after which the property was to descend to Allen and he was required then to pay yearly the sum of £5 to his mother, Elizabeth. Allen senior left his second son, William, his tenement and 4 acres of land in the parish of Foxton when William attained the age of 24 years. William also received £40 and daughters Susan, Annabel, Martha, Mary and Sara each received £80 of *lawfull money of England*. There is no mention of lands or farms but the sums involved indicate a moderate degree of wealth. Allen also signed his name which indicates he could read and write. It is difficult to estimate what these amounts would equate to in today's money but £80 might be equivalent to about £15,000–20,000 today. Finally, it is interesting to speculate that the house in Foxton left to William may have been the house built by or for Thomas around 1600.

In her will, Elizabeth seems to have been particularly concerned with her daughter, Annabel. Much of the will is taken up with instructions to give money and goods (bed and bedding) to Annabel, but places responsibility for Annabel's maintenance with her son-in-law, Henry Greenhill (the husband of Mary). After the death of Annabel the money was to be divided equally between sons Allen and William, and daughters Susannah (married to Henry Lilly), Martha (married to Jacob Hawkes) and Sarah. Sarah, or Sara, was made sole Executrix. However the main interest of Elizabeth's will for us is the inventory of her goods and chattels drawn up after her death on 5 July 1671. The full list is given in Appendix 4, which shows she was quite well off.

It is not known whether these goods were in the house in Sible Hedingham but the inventory indicates a house with seven rooms: chamber, room over the parlour, parlour, kitchen, dairy, buttery and chamber over the dairy. The total goods were valued at £166 10s which in today's money might be worth £30,000.

Annabel's will, signed with her mark on 20 March 1685, in her turn gave back £15 to each of the children of her benefactor Henry Greenhill: Elizabeth, Mary, Jane, Frances, Henry and William. The inventory of her goods and chattels shows that she did not have much apart from some wearing apparel, bed and bedding but she did have £80 in a box. Could this be the £80 left to Annabel in her father's will, still unspent? Two other wills from this period are relevant: The eldest son Allen who married Jane Greenhill, apart from inheriting directly from his father, was the recipient of an inheritance from his sister Martha and mentioned in the will of father-in-law John Greenhill. In 1695, after leaving money to her sisters and brother William and their children, Martha Hawkes finished by giving... *unto my loving brother Mr Allen Hurrell of Newton and to his heires forever All my lands tenements & heriditaments with their appurtenances...* John Greenhill of Sawston, in 1677, left £20 each to his grandchildren, including the children of Allen and Jane. Furthermore, Jane received £5 as well. The above lands and tenements were the nucleus of a private estate which was passed on to the next two generations.

Allen's sister Sarah married Nathaniel Singleton on 28 March 1676 in St. Michael's, Cambridge and went to live in Foxton. Nathaniel had just inherited from his father leases on the rectory and the Bury demesne totalling 400 acres. Both these were later occupied by the Hurrells. Nathaniel may have been a Dissenter, as Rowland Parker has recorded that in 1685 the 'free-thinkers' numbered thirty-nine who were holding meetings in Nathaniel Singleton's great barn at Mortimer's.

During this period the discontent among some of the population with the established church which had been building over the 17th century began to take form. Those separating from the Church of England, called Dissenters, gradually organised themselves into the separate denominations of Presbyterians, Congregationalists and Baptists. Those who remained in the Church but who were unhappy with many of its doctrines were called Nonconformists and by the early 18th century came to be known as the Low Church part of the Church of England. From this point on these groups are encountered more frequently in the villages of Newton, Harston and Foxton. Through the 17th century many villagers became apathetic about the Church and the churches in some villages fell into disrepair.

This generation lived through the turbulent years of the 17th century, particularly the English Civil War of the 1640s, culminating in the execution of King Charles I in 1649. This was followed by the Commonwealth then the 'Protectorate', dominated by Oliver Cromwell, which in turn ended with the Restoration of the monarchy and the arrival of Charles II in 1660. Charles was succeeded by his brother, James II, in 1665 and the disputes and dissent and suspicions began again which led to the 'Glorious Revolution' of 1688 when James was exiled and William and Mary of the Netherlands were invited to take the throne on conditions which finally established the supremacy of Parliament. The Civil War between the Royalists and Parliamentarians (Cavaliers and Roundheads) was waged the length of England (and also in Ireland and Scotland) but no major battle was fought near the villages of Harston, Foxton and Newton so that the Hurrells probably were not much affected by it. Whether any of the villagers were pressed into the army on either side is not known; but Rowland Parker records that for a time Cromwell's gunners were billeted in Foxton.

We can speculate as to which side the Hurrells supported. The evidence from the wills suggests that they were supporters of the local Anglican parish church and Anglicans, along with the majority of landowners, were generally supporters of the Royalists. However, there were no hard and fast rules. Probably, what concerned them more at this time were the three consecutive bad harvests of 1647–9.

* * * * *

Children of Allen Hurrell, Jane Greehill and Anne (unknown)

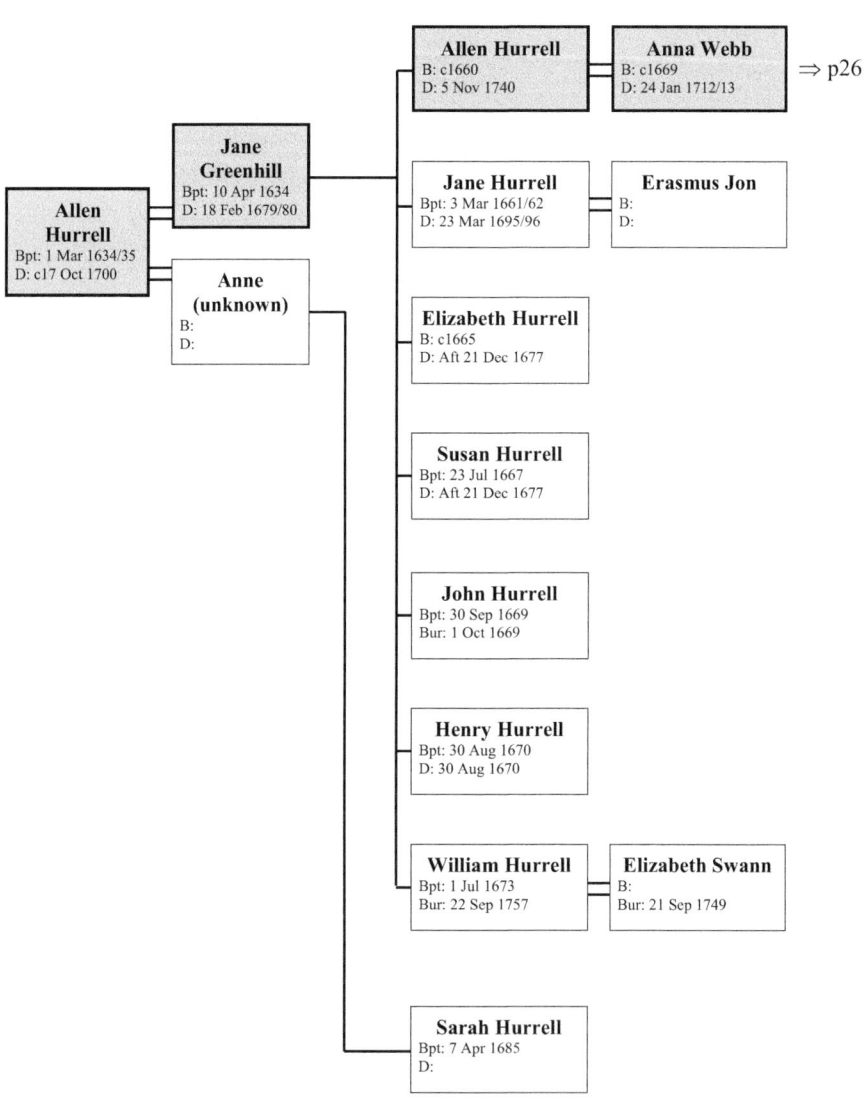

Chapter 4

Newton, Cambridgeshire

Son Allen, who was baptised on 16 March 1635 in Harston, was first married to Jane (or Jeane) Greenhill on 19 July 1660 in St Mary The Great, Cambridge. Jane, who was born in Sawston and was baptised on 10 April 1634, was the daughter of John Greenhill and Jane Biatt. The family settled in Newton where all seven children were born between 1660 and 1673. Two boys, John and Henry, died in infancy and Jane died and was buried on 18 February 1680. Allen then married again, someone called Anne, and they had one child, Sarah, who was baptised on 7 April 1685 in Newton.

Allen died and was buried on 17 October 1700 in Newton. Allen's will was signed with his mark on 3 February 1698. By this time it is obvious that his estate had grown to include freehold and copyhold lands in Newton, Hauxton and Harston. He commenced by leaving his second wife, Anne, all the freehold lands and tenements with appurtenances which had been lately purchased from William and Mary Etheridge for the term of Anne's natural life. Then these lands were to go to Sarah, her daughter, and her heirs. Anne also received a bed, bedding, curtains, chairs and stools. The eldest son, Allen, was left all the copyhold lands and tenements in the towns and fields of Newton, Hauxton and Harston. Martha Hawkes' *lands, tenements and heriditaments with their appurtenances* given to Allen were split between Anne, his wife, and Elizabeth and Sarah, his daughters. Anne got the house or tenement held of St Peter's College, Cambridge, which was to pass to sons Allen and William on her death. Three houses or tenements held of Benet College, Cambridge, were given jointly to Elizabeth and Sarah for their natural life and heirs. If there were no heirs then they would pass to Allen.

A surprise was the freehold lands with appurtenances in Harston containing 21 acres which had been given to Allen by his brother-in-law, John Greenhill, and was in turn passed on to his son William. These lands must have been given to Allen at some stage after John Greenhill's will of 1677 as it is not mentioned in that will.

William also received £500, Elizabeth £200 and each of daughter Jane Jon and her husband Erasmus's four children, Allen, John, Joseph and Robert received £20. Jane had died on 16 March 1696, two years before Allen's will. Finally, all the rest of the goods, chattels and personal estate after debts, legacies and funeral charges were left jointly to Allen and William who were made joint Executors. £500 in today's money might be worth in the order of £70,000.

Sons, Allen, married to Anna Webb, and William, who married Elizabeth Swann, were the progenitors of two major branches in the Hurrell line. In about 1718, William acquired the lease on Newton Bury, and his descendants established what might be called a dynasty in Newton and Harston. Allen's descendants went on to settle in Foxton – of which more later.

In *British History Online* for the parishes of Hauxton and Newton, William is described as a prosperous local farmer who also occupied the rectory under his brother-in-law Robert Swann, then its lessee. William died in 1757 and the Bury lease, to which much land was added by purchase, descended to William's son (died 1779), grandson (died 1830) and great-grandson (died 1854), all named William. About 1840, William (died 1854) and his son William between them owned about 330 acres in Newton and occupied over 300 acres more including the Bury farm. The last-named William we shall meet again as William Hurrell of Newton, one of the Executors of the will in the infamous Chancery case.

In the Name of God Amen Allen Purcell of Newton in the County of Cambridge Yeoman Doe make this my last Will & Testament touching my temporall estate as followeth first I give & bequeath all my ffreeholds Lands & Tenements with their appurtenances lying & being within the parish of Newton aforesaid & Hauxton & Barston in the said County with the Hatch pightle &c of William Elleridge Moore his wife, unto Anne my loveing wife for & dureing her naturall life (in lieu of dower) & from & after the death of my said wife I doe give & bequeath the said Lands & Tenements with th'appurtenances unto my daughter Sarah Purcell & her heires Item I give & bequeath unto my sonn William Purcell & his heires All those my ffreehold Lands with their appurtenances lying in Hauxton aforesaid conteining by estimation one & twenty acres be the same more or lesse which were given & devised to me by my ffather by his Guift in Land in severall great doreases Item I give to my said sonn William Purcell five hundred pounds of lawfull money of England to be paid within one yeare after my decease Item I give & bequeath unto my daughter Elizabeth Purcell the sume of Two hundred pounds of lawfull money of England to be paid within six months after my decease Item I give & bequeath unto my daughter Susan of the money of England to be paid within one yeare after my decease Item I give & bequeath unto the said Anne my wife one wrought bed with all Irons thereto with the Carved Cubbard & bedstead & bedding thereto therein & the houshold stuffe hereunto belonging Item I give & bequeath unto my said wife All that messuage or Tenement wherein I now dwell & the Masters ffellowes & Schollars of St Bennett Colledge in the University of Cambridge within & hath of the gift & bequest of my sister Martha Pauncefoote of Crane Goden aforesaid widow decease, now in the occupacon of Mr Abraham Baker situate lying & being in Trumpeth parish in Cambridge aforesaid for & dureing the tearme of her naturall life she paying the Colledge rent as it shall become due for the same After that decease I give the said Messuage or Tenement unto my two sonns Allen Purcell & William Purcell their heires & Assignes for ever Item I give & bequeath unto my said daughters Elizabeth & Sarah All those my Messuages or Tenements within were lately given & devised to me now by the last Will & Testament of my said sister Martha Pauncefoote late of the Masters ffellowes & Schollars of Bennett Colledge in the University of Cambridge aforesaid now in the occupacon of Mr Newton Mr Williams & Mr Hippey situate lying & being in the parish of St Bennett in Cambridge aforesaid for & during the tearme of their naturall lives & after their deceases & decease then I give the said Messuages & tenements to the heires of them & either of them lawfully to be begotten, And for & if it shall happen that the said Elizabeth & Sarah shall depart this life without issue of them or either of them bodies & lawful begotten then I give the said Messuages or Tenements unto my said sonn Allen Purcell & his heires & Assignes for ever And my mind & will is that my said daughters shall pay unto Elizabeth Wonton of Cambridge aforesaid widow the sume of foure pounds of lawfull money of England yearly dureing her naturall life to be paid quarterly at twenty shillings a quarter, Item I give unto my sonn Allen Purcell All my Coppihold Lands & Tenements lying in the towne fields of Newton & Hauxton & Barston aforesaid, Item I give & bequeath unto the foure Children of my daughter Anne Fron Martha Foxley Alice Fron John Fron Joseph Fron Robert Fron Twenty pounds apeice to be paid unto them when they shall attaine to their severall ages of one & twenty yeares Item I give unto the poore of the parish of Newton aforesaid twenty shillings Item I give & bequeath unto my said wife five pounds to buy her mourning All the rest of my goods Chattells & personall estate after my debts payed and funerall charges paid I give & bequeath unto my said sonns Allen Purcell & William Purcell whome I doe make & appoint sole Executors of this my last Will & testament In witness whereof I have hereunto sett my hand & seale this the — day of ffebruary in the twenty yeare of the Reigne of our Soveraigne Lord William the third by the grace of God of England, Scotland, ffrance & Ireland, King Defender of the faith &c Annoq Dni 1698.

Signed sealed published & declared by the
said Allen Purcell the Testator as for
his last Will & Testament in the presence of
us whose names are subscribed

James ffletcher
Thomas Bies
his [mark]

Memorand that I doe give the sume of fifty
pounds Anne Fron, save the said
[...] Colledge [...]

Allen Purcell

A true & perfect Inventory of all ye Goods and Chattels of Allen Hurrell of Newton in ye County of Cambridge yeoman taken & appraised by us whose names are underwritten this fifteenth day of October 1700

	£ – s – d
Imprimis for his wearing Apparell & money in his purse	20 – 00 – 00
Item in ye Hall Chamber one bed with bedding & Chaires belonging to itt with other Lumber	09 – 10 – 00
Item in ye Little Chamber over ye Parler one bedd with Chaires belonging to itt with other Lumber	06 – 00 – 00
Item in ye Parlor Chamber three beds with other Lumber	10 – 00 – 00
Item ye Maids Chamber one bed	01 – 00 – 00
Item in ye Garrett ould Lumber	01 – 05 – 00
Item in ye Parlor one Clock two tables 13 Chaires one Looking glas with other Lumber	06 – 10 – 00
Item in ye Hall 3 tables 11 Chaires with other Lumber	02 – 15 – 00
Item in ye Kitchin one Jack with Chaires & other Lumber	02 – 05 – 06
Item for Poulter	04 – 15 – 04
Item for brass Coppers & brewing vessels	08 – 03 – 04
Item in ye Dary one Cheesepres & Churn with other Lumber	02 – 03 – 00
Item for a parsell of Cheese	05 – 00 – 00
Item for a Coughtin mill with other Lumber	01 – 00 – 00
Item for 3 flock beds in ye Servants Chamber	01 – 10 – 00
Item in ye Sellar hogsheads & barrells with other Lumber	03 – 04 – 00
Item for Sheets & napkins & other wearing Linin	09 – 10 – 00
Item for one Silver tankerd	06 – 10 – 00
Item for 40 hogs & pigs	20 – 18 – 08
Item for 21 Cowes & a bull	51 – 06 – 08
Item for a parsell of wooll	20 – 00 – 00
Item for nine horses & their harneses	78 – 15 – 00
Item for one wagon & fowr Carts	20 – 00 – 00
Item for ploughs harrows & rouls with other Lumber	04 – 00 – 00
Item for Sacks & Screen & bushell with other Lumber	03 – 10 – 00
Item for a parsell of hay	11 – 00 – 00
Item for a parsell of Lintills in ye Straw	13 – 00 – 00
Item for a parsell of pease in Straw	30 – 00 – 00
Item for a parsell of Rie & wheat in ye Garner	04 – 10 – 00
Item for a parsell of oats in ye Straw	03 – 04 – 00
Item for fifteen score & nine Sheep	103 – 05 – 00
Item for ploughing of 70 acres of Tyth & times	28 – 09 – 04
Item for 14 quarters of wheat to sow itt	21 – 00 – 00
Item for 20 acres ploughing three times	11 – 01 – 00
Item for nine quarters of English to sow itt	09 – 00 – 00
Item for ploughing of sixty acres of Tyth twise	17 – 00 – 00
Item for Carridg of dung & mud	05 – 00 – 00
Item for ploughing of 20 acres of Stubbles	03 – 00 – 00
Item for barly in ye Straw	221 – 00 – 00
Item for meslin in ye Straw	50 – 00 – 00
Item for wheat in ye Straw	77 – 00 – 00
Item for debts good & desperett	250 – 00 – 00

Wm Stevenson
John Sergeant

The Hurrells of Newton twice crossed over in cousin marriages with the descendants of Allen and Anna to maintain a close relationship. Some of the copyhold land held of the Ely manor in Hauxton and Newton was bought by the Hurrells of Harston soon after the 1660s (probably by Allen and Jane), which was passed to eldest son Allen in the will of 1698. Also, part of that inheritance it seems was the impropriate rectory held of Jesus College, Cambridge, under the Bishop of Ely long occupied by Allen Hurrell and his descendants. *British History Online* mentions that these Hurrells had a substantial private estate, partly inherited in 1693 (1698?) and enlarged by 1800 to cover 197 acres. Allen (died 1740) was succeeded by son Allen (died 1745) upon whose widow Margaret's death in 1762 the lease and land passed to their daughter, Margaret's husband, John Bridge (died 1776), and his heirs.

Allen and Jane brought up their children in a time of stirring events. Although not directly affected they must have been alarmed and concerned with the Great Plague of London when 100,000 people died in 1665. This was followed in 1666 by the Fire of London which surely would have caused shock and disbelief. It was a time also of developments in science and new inventions, which perhaps were only of passing interest. In 1687 Sir Isaac Newton stated his laws of motion and the theory of gravitation followed by the publication of his Opticks in 1704. In 1712 Thomas Newcomen invented the first practical steam engine and in 1733 John Kay invented the flying shuttle or weaving machine. Politically too there were developments: after the Glorious Revolution, William and Mary were crowned in 1689 along with a Bill of Rights which gave citizens certain rights including the right to petition the Monarch and the right to bear arms for defence whilst also limiting the Monarch's freedom to act without agreement by Parliament. In 1707 The Act of Union joined England and Scotland in one country. Two abortive attempts to put the clock back and restore the Stuarts to the throne failed in the Jacobite rebellions of 1715 and 1745.

* * * * *

Children of Allen Hurrell and Anna Webb

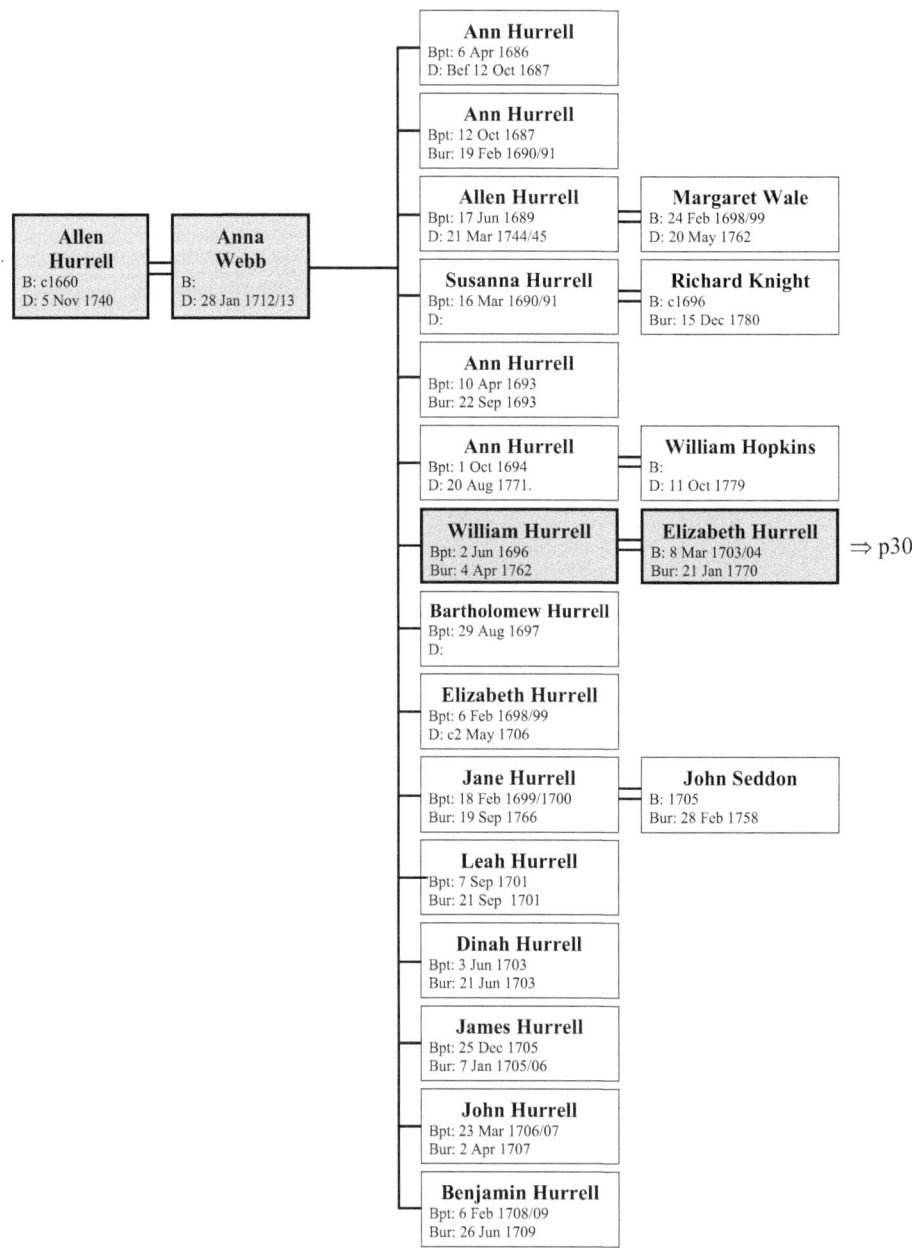

Chapter 5

Back to Harston

Allen, born about 1660, married Anna Webb of Gamlingay, Cambridgeshire, on 17 February 1685 at Croxton, Cambridgeshire. Their first five children were born in Sawston but of these only two survived, three girls all named Ann dying in infancy. The family then moved to Harston where the remaining ten children were born. Again, five of these ten died in infancy, two girls and three boys and Elizabeth died at the age of seven. This is an appalling rate of infant mortality and speaks volumes of the resolution of the family to keep going in the face of adversity. During the period in Sawston, Allen was the Rector and occupied Brooke House. Anna died 24 January 1713 and was buried in Harston. So far as is known Allen did not marry again.

On 12 January 1719, the eldest son, Allen the younger, married Margaret Wale, daughter of Gregory Wale and Margaret Spark, and they had ten children. Allen died in 1745 and we have seen that the lands he inherited from his father passed to Margaret's heirs. Our line descends from the second son, William, who married Elizabeth Hurrell, the first of the cousin marriages.

Chapter 5

Of the other siblings, Susanna, or Susan, married Richard Knight and went to live in Foxton. Richard, a yeoman farmer, died in Foxton and was buried at the age of 84 years on 15 December 1780. The following year, estate agents in Royston put up Richard Knight's house and farm in Foxton for sale.

Ann, born 1694, married William Hopkins who was the Vicar of Elmdon from 1720 to 1779, the year he died. They raised eight children in Elmdon, which lies a few miles south of Foxton, just over the Cambridge/Essex border.

St Nicholas' Church, Elmdon, Essex.

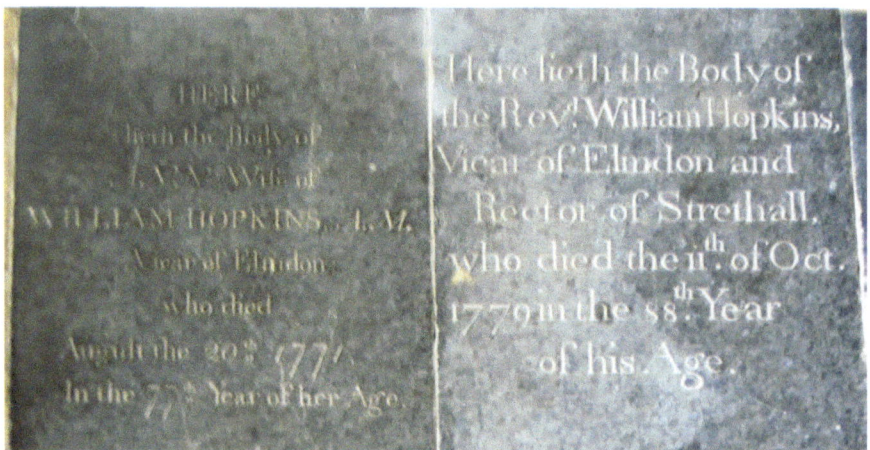

Elmdon Church, floor plaques of William Hopkins and his wife, Anna.

Jane married John Seddon and also lived in Foxton. John was buried in Foxton on 28 February 1758 whereas Jane was buried on 19 September 1766 in Harston.

Allen the elder signed his will on 10 December 1736 in Harston. Apart from a house or tenement called the Swann situated in Harston with some arable land, meadow and pasture given to his son William, the main part of his estate including houses and tenements as well as freehold and copyhold lands were given as we have seen to the eldest son Allen, which later passed to Margaret's heirs. Jane received all the household linen and all the household goods and furniture, and Allen received all the rest of his goods and chattels and personal estate, but Allen was charged with the payment of his debts, legacies and funeral expenses. In addition to all this, Ann and her brother, William, received £300 each, Jane received £600 and Susan received £20. The poor of Harston were given forty shillings to be distributed. Allen was made the sole Executor. £300 in today's money might be worth about £26,000. It should be noted that at the time Allen's will was drawn up, Jane was not married.

At the beginning of the 18th century England was a sparsely populated agricultural country. The total population of England was about five million in 1700. Three quarters of the population lived in rural areas in small village communities. Diseases, such as measles, smallpox and influenza were frequent childhood afflictions and high infant mortality was a common occurrence although not generally as high as in this family. The average life expectancy at birth was only about 35 years. The incidence of some diseases over time lessened, for instance, bubonic plague was not known in England after 1667. Inoculation against smallpox was introduced about 1720 and thereafter it declined in importance.

Poor harvests in 1710, 1727, 1728 and 1740 led to high prices and distress among the labouring classes and must have affected farmers' returns. The average annual income of a labourer in 1700 varied from just over £11 in Lancashire to £25 in London (perhaps £1,000 to £3,000 in today's money). We have no comparable subsistence wages in the western world today but wives and families often added considerably to these incomes by labour in the fields. For comparison, the average income per family in agriculture was £50–£60 with the bigger farmers, such as the Hurrells earning considerably more.

* * * * *

Children of William Hurrell and Elizabeth Hurrell

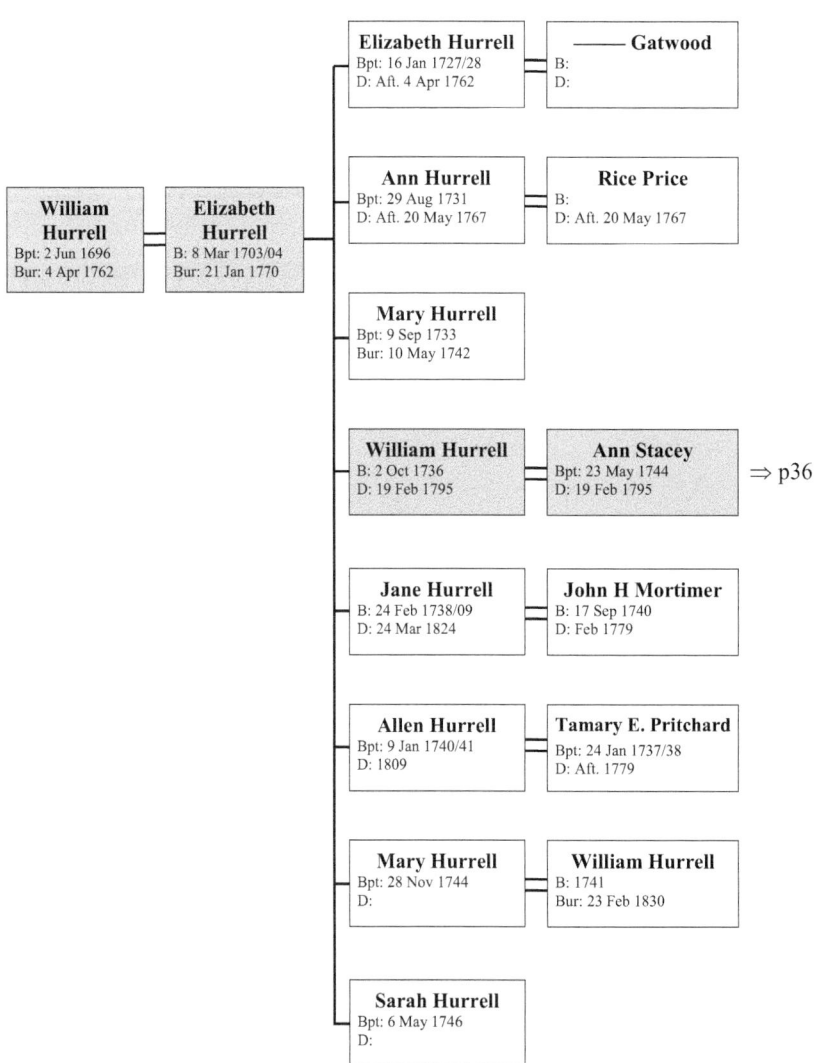

⇒ p36

Chapter 6

Foxton, Cambridgeshire

William Hurrell, the son of Allen Hurrell and Anna Webb, who was baptised on 2 June 1696 in Harston, married Elizabeth Hurrell on 20 May 1727 in Elmdon, Essex, by the vicar, William Hopkins, his sister's husband. Elizabeth was William's first cousin, the daughter of William Hurrell and Elizabeth Swann from the previous generation. It was Elizabeth's brother William and his wife Ann Smith who continued the dynasty in Newton. Elizabeth was born on 8 March 1704 in Newton and was baptised on 16 March. Soon after their marriage the couple settled in Foxton, becoming tenants under John Welbore by 1727. Eight children were born in Foxton between 1728 and 1746. By 1743 they had occupied the Bury farm and the rectory, tenancies that had previously been held by Nathaniel Singleton. From then the Hurrells continued to occupy the Bury for nearly one hundred years.

The first born, Elizabeth, who was baptised on 16 January 1728, married a man named Gatwood and moved to London between 1760 and 1765. The second born, Ann, baptised on 29 August 1731, married Rice Price, a

Chapter 6

Haberdasher, on the 26 August 1763 at St Paul's, Covent Garden, and also lived in London.

The third child Mary, baptised on 9 September 1733, died at the age of eight and was buried in Newton on the 10 May 1742. The fourth child William, who married Ann Stacey, is our immediate ancestor on this family tree and more about him later. He was followed by Jane who married John Hamilton Mortimer, a well-known artist who became president of the Society of Artists in 1774 and joined the Royal Academy in 1778. Jane was born on 24 February 1739. She married John on 11 February 1775 in St Paul's Church, Covent Garden, London. John was born on 17 September 1740 in Eastbourne, Sussex. Amongst his many projects, he designed the east window of Salisbury

Jane Mortimer (née Hurrell).

John H Mortimer, self-portrait.

Cathedral and painted the ceiling of the entrance hall of Brocket Hall, Herts. It is said that John's haphazard life changed for the better after his marriage to Jane. However, the marriage was short lived as John died in February 1779 at the age of 38 and was buried at High Wycombe. Jane lived on to the age of 85; she was buried at Eastbourne on 31 March 1824. In his will, John left all his estate and effects, real and personal, to his dearly beloved wife.

The sixth child, Allen Hurrell, baptised 9 January 1741, married Tamary Elizabeth Pritchard on 23 September 1769 in St Clement Danes Church, Westminster, London. They had two children, Mary Ann and John Forbes. Tamary, who was baptised 24 January 1738, was the daughter of William and Hannah Pritchard (née Vaughan) both actors. Tamary herself became the author of six 'tales of imagination' printed in London in two volumes. In the late 1760s Tamary lived in Ragman's Castle, which had been purchased by the Pritchards, a well-known house at the time on Twickenham Riverside at the corner of Orleans House estate. It is not known what Allen did in his career.

Seventh was Mary, baptised 28 November 1744, who married William Hurrell of Newton on 30 October 1766 at Harston, the second of the cousin marriages. William died in 1830 and was buried in Newton. He was the son of William Hurrell and Ann Smith and helped to renew the close relationship between the two sides of the family. Mary and William had three children, William, Swan and Smith. The eldest, William (died 1854), was the father of William the Younger (died 1902), the trustee in the Chancery case.

The eighth and last child, Sarah, was baptised on 6 May 1746 in Foxton; there is nothing further known about her.

As far as is known, William who married Elizabeth Hurrell left no will. He was buried in Harston on 4 April 1762. Elizabeth's brother William of Newton, who signed his will on 20 May 1767, left her £10 and gave £5 to the children: William, Allen, Elizabeth Gatward (*sic*) widow, Ann Price and Jane Hurrell. William of Newton was buried 6 July 1779, and the will was proved on 8 February 1781. Elizabeth was buried on 21 January 1770 in Foxton so presumably her £10 was passed to her children. Of those not mentioned, we must presume that Sarah died before 1767 and Mary who married William (died 1830) was taken care of well.

The mid-years of the 18th century saw the expansion of the British Empire in India and Canada (Battle of Quebec 1759) during the Seven Years' War with France. Captain Cook started his voyages of discovery in 1768. The Stuarts were replaced on the throne by the Hanoverian dynasty starting with George I in 1714 and continuing with George II in 1727 and George III in 1760. England remained a largely rural and agricultural country and, as before, the years of bad harvests and high prices in 1751, 1756 and 1766 would have been of more immediate interest to the Hurrells of Foxton and Newton.

* * * * *

Children of William Hurrell and Ann Stacey

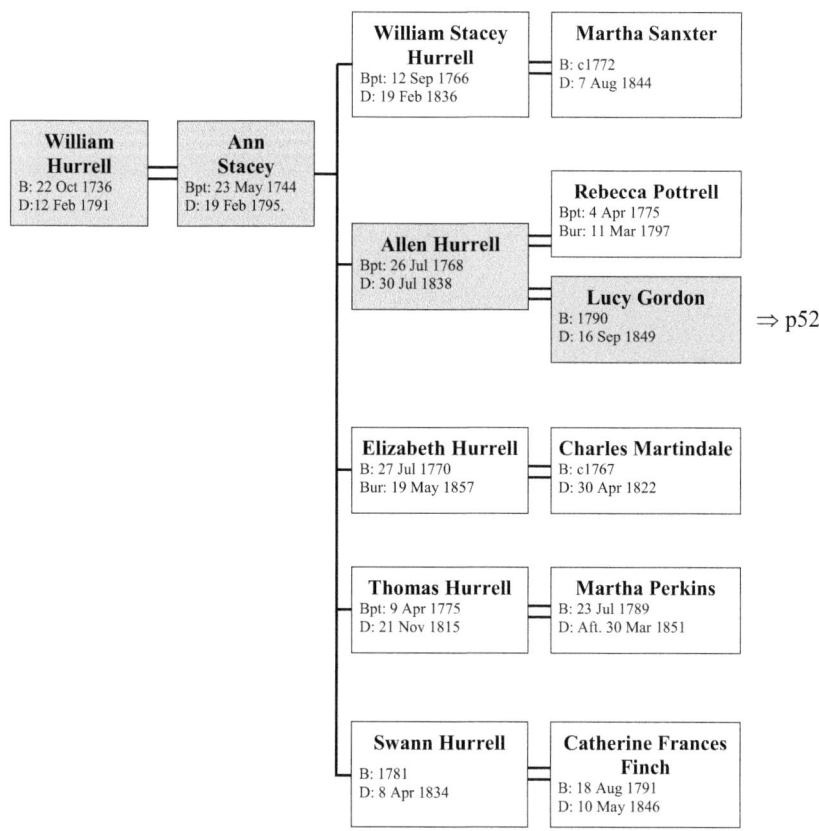

Chapter 7

Foxton, Next Generation

William (the Major's great grandfather) was born on 22 October 1736 in Foxton. He married Ann Stacey on 12 September 1765 in Foxton. Ann was baptised on 23 May 1744 in Trumpington, Cambridgeshire. In 1743, at the age of seven, William moved into the Bury farm house with his parents and five of his brothers and sisters, as tenant farmers. Foxton Bury was on the site of the ancient 'hall' of the manor owned by the Abbess of Chatteris before the dissolution of the monasteries. The hall was the meeting place of the manor court. The present building was built for Sir Richard Warren in 1593 and continued for a time to be the hall of the manor for public meetings. After many changes of ownership, the Bury farm was purchased by the Bendyshe family in 1787. Over the years it was added to and altered, partly by William.

By this time the Hurrells, both in Foxton and Newton, were beginning to acquire land and profit from farming. It is noticeable that as time progressed they regarded themselves as elevated in status. No longer yeoman, the male Hurrells in wills began to refer to themselves as 'gentleman' and in the next generation those occupying Foxton Bury and Newton Bury referred to themselves as 'Esquire', even though neither family owned these manors.

Chapter 7

They still lived on their farms and farmed the land, sometimes through bailiffs, but along with their increased status the Hurrells also accepted responsibility for others. Rowland Parker records how William served as a parish official for most of his adult life, either as Overseer or Churchwarden and sometimes both, answerable to the Vestry. He was also able to provide employment for half the village. To quote Rowland Parker:

Above: Foxton Bury, as it is today. The building, other than the main 'hall', was altered and enlarged, mainly by the Hurrells.

Right: Foxton Bury, as it may have looked in the 18th century when first lived in by William and Ann Hurrell.

> ...he provided four fifths of the money doled out to the poor; he lent money free of interest to many old people. Other men in Hurrell's class were spending their time and money in trying to rise higher in the social scale for the gratification of their own vanity and ambition, to achieve which they had to migrate to such places as London, Bath, Cheltenham and Harrogate. He saw fit to stay in, and serve, his own village. Many, very many men in England had less justification for a clear conscience than William Hurrell of Foxton.

It was probably about this time or a generation later, along with their raised standing in the community, that the Hurrells adopted their coat of arms, mentioned in the Major's letter at the beginning of this history. Many people at the time were doing the same. The Hurrell arms are documented in Burke's *General Armory* (1878 edition) and, even earlier, the Hurrell arms (that is the shield) are mentioned in the *Vale Royall of England* by Daniel King, 1656. The shield alone appears emblazoned on a wall of Park House, Harston, which was built by Henry Hurrell in 1854; the crest alone was engraved on the back of a gold fob watch belonging to the Major; there was also a signet ring engraved with the crest. The General Armory does not indicate in the case of Hurrell to whom the coat of arms was first granted and there are no illustrations. The description covers the shield and the crest but there is no mention of the helmet or decorative fronds (mantling).

The Hurrell coat of arms.

These items, the shape of the shield and the scroll appear to be standard additions as exactly the same items have been seen on arms of another family. In his description, the Major mistook the crossbows for bows and arrows and the claim that they represented the name quarrel (from which he derived Hurrell), a famous shooter in the *Domesday Book*, cannot be substantiated. His reference to a canting coat of arms alludes to the representation of the 'famous shooter' by the weapons (crossbows). Perhaps it is worth adding that crossbows were never much used in England where the longbow was favoured because of its greater range and rate of fire. They were, however, used in France.

William and Ann had five children between 1766 and 1781. The first child was baptised William Stacey Hurrell on 12 September 1766 in Foxton. On the 21 March 1796, he married Martha Sanxter at Witcham, Cambridgeshire.

Chapter 7

After his father died, he took over the farms in Foxton parish and continued to live at Foxton Bury.

Allen, grandfather of the Major, was born in 1768 in Foxton and baptised on 26 July 1770, the day before his younger sister, Elizabeth. More of him later.

The third child, Elizabeth, was baptised on 27 July 1770 in Foxton. She married Charles Martindale on 7 June 1791 in Foxton. Charles was born, place unknown, in about 1767. The couple lived in Sawston and had seven children where Charles was in turn a farmer, solicitor and entrepreneur. Charles died at the age of 55 years and was buried on 6 May 1822 in Sawston. Elizabeth lived to the age of 87 years; she was buried on 19 May 1857 in Sawston. The couple's eldest child, Charles William Martindale, became a paper manufacturer at Sawston Mills and married Ann, the daughter of William Stacey Hurrell and Martha Sanxter (another cousin marriage).

The fourth child, Thomas, was baptised on 9 April 1775 in Foxton. He married Martha Perkins on 2 April 1811 in Arkesden, Essex, where she had been born on 23 July 1789. They lived in Chrishall Hall, Essex, where he was buried on 21 November 1815 aged 44 years. They had two children. Thomas made a will, proved in 1816, which left all the lands and estates purchased by him from Lord Braybrooke in Arkesden to his brother Allen, provided Allen paid for them! By this time Allen had acquired land at Arkesden through his first wife, Rebecca Pottrell, and there is no evidence he ever took up the offer.

The fifth and last child was Swann Hurrell born about 1781 in Foxton. He married Catherine Frances Finch on 9 December 1811 in Little Shelford, Cambridgeshire. Catherine was born 18 August 1791 in Cambridge. During their married life the couple raised five children in Cambridge. One son, Charles Hurrell, emigrated to New Zealand where he died in August 1840. A daughter, Anne, who married the Reverend John Dawson Gibson, died in Bombay, India, in 1850 aged 28. The second son, also named Swann, was born in 1816 and lived to the age of 81 becoming a prominent Cambridge personality. In 1847, he took over the Finch family business in Market Hill and Iron Foundry at Bridge Street from his uncle, Charles Finch. As a result he became known to the family as the Iron Duke. He served as an alderman and was elected Mayor of Cambridge in 1856, 1857 and from 1864 to 1866. He was the author of the *Swann Hurrell Manuscript*, written in the 1890s,

Altar and Chancel of Foxton Church. The Chancel contains the gravestones of William Hurrell (d.1791), Ann Hurrell (née Stacey) (d.1795), Thomas Hurrell (d.1815), Swann Hurrell (d.1834), William Stacey Hurrell (d.1836), Martha Hurrell (née Sanxter) (d.1844), Catherine Hurrell (née Finch) (d.1846) as well as other Hurrell descendants.

Chapter 7

Foxton Church in 2011.

possibly the first attempt to delve into the family history of the Hurrells. He was a cousin of Major William Hurrell's father and it was he who asked to meet the Major after hearing of his exploits in Rhodesia in 1896.

William (died 12 February, 1791), his wife Ann (died 19 February 1795), William Stacey (died 20 January 1836), his wife Martha (died 7 August 1844), Thomas (died November 1815) Swann (died 2 April 1834) and his wife Catherine (died 10 May 1846) were all buried in the Chancel of Foxton Church. Allen (died 30 July 1838) and his second wife Lucy (died 17 September 1849) were buried in the grounds of Arkesden Church and as already mentioned Elizabeth (died May 1857) and her husband Charles (died 30 April 1822) were buried in Sawston.

William Hurrell: burial plaque in the floor in the Chancel at Foxton Church.

On 18 September 1779, William and his brothers-in-law, William Stacey of Newton and Thomas Stacey of Trumpington (both farmers) were bound to the 'Worshipful William Compton Doctor of Laws Chancellor of the Diocese of Ely' in the sum of £400 on condition that William would administer fairly and make a 'true and perfect Inventory' of the 'Goods, Chattles and Credits' of his mother, Elizabeth, who had died intestate in 1770. The result of his administration was to be completed by the last day of August 1780 and the proceeds would then be delivered and paid to such persons as the judge or judges of the Consistory Court of the Lord Bishop of Ely would appoint. What the goods, chattels and credits were is not revealed. In today's money the surety of £400 would be worth about £28,000, a substantial sum of money.

In 1775, William owned only 9 acres in Foxton but was leasing 308 acres of the Bury, Bendyshe and Hatton estates. From this time, William and later his son, William Stacey Hurrell began to build up and accumulate an estate of their own. According to Rowland Parker, at their peak the Hurrells farmed about 800 acres of their own and leased land. Ownership of land not only gave status but also political influence and the right to vote in parliamentary elections. Rowland Parker also quotes the press report at the time of a disastrous fire in 1788 that started in a barn of William Hurrell's and destroyed several houses in the east end of the village.

Meanwhile in Newton, the Newton Hurrells were doing much the same. William (died 1779) and his son William (died 1830) continued to farm the Newton Bury lease and began to accumulate an estate in Newton and Harston of their own.

The middle half of the 18th century was a good time to live in rural England for all but the poorest. The land produced more than the population needed. The drift to the towns and the impacts of the Napoleonic Wars and the protectionism, that ultimately failed in the early 19th century, were as yet over the horizon. Swathes of Cambridgeshire were prosperous wheat growing country at the time. All this must have had a bearing on William at the Bury in Foxton, glowingly praised for his caring attitude to the less fortunate locals in the village by Rowland Parker.

By mid-century the population of England and Wales was still only about seven million people and the country was mainly rural and agricultural. The

Chapter 7

land Enclosure movement accelerated after 1760 but did not affect Foxton and Newton until later. Three quarters of the population lived in village communities. There were few large towns, London being the exception. By mid-century it already had a population of about 700,000 and was the largest town in Europe. The journalist Daniel Defoe in 1726 argued that the country enjoyed a national economy which originated with and was sustained by the demands of London for consumer goods including food. By 1770 about 15,000 miles of trunk roads connecting London with the major centres had been turnpiked and travelling was becoming much easier, though expensive. The population of Foxton was somewhere between 200 and 300 inhabitants, mostly farm labourers. The average annual income of agricultural workers had hardly changed since the beginning of the century, increasing from about £18 to £25. Throughout this period there was a population drift from the south to the north to serve the development of metal industries in the Midlands and the cotton trade in Lancashire.

Where do the Hurrells fit in the social scale at this time in the second half of the 18th century? Geoffrey Alderman in 'Modern Britain 1700 – 1983' said that the great landlords, who included the peerage, had incomes in excess of £3,000; the remainder of the gentry, which would have included the Hurrells, had annual incomes ranging from £300 to £3,000. These amounts in today's money would be around £24,000 to £240,000. Possibly, at this stage of their development, the Hurrells would have been in the middle to lower end of the range. According to Alderman, a petty bourgeois family would have considered £100 a very solid income which today would be approximately equivalent to £8,000.

The 18th century brought in more intensive methods of farming and new techniques, such as the introduction of turnips and clover into crop rotations, improvements in livestock breeding and the use of manure as fertiliser. The seed drill was invented by Jethro Tull in 1701 and a machine for the threshing of corn made its appearance in Scotland in 1758. As always, economies of scale meant that the larger farmers prospered and the small freeholder found it hard to compete.

Particularly in London, newspapers were becoming quite common so that, living not far from Cambridge, world news probably filtered through. The

Gordon riots in 1780 in London, in which an anti-Catholic mob of 60,000 had to be brought under control by the army with the loss of some 290 lives and several hundred injured, would have caused a stir even in the country. But by far the most momentous events were taking place across the Atlantic. The Boston Tea Party in 1773 led to the Declaration of Independence of the 13 American colonies in 1776 followed by the American War of Independence and the loss of the American colonies. Two years before William died the French Revolution began in 1789, but he did not live to see the consequences of that.

* * *

Both William Stacey Hurrell and his brother, Allen grew up in Foxton Bury (see chart page 36). We are not told where they went to school but probably in Cambridge. William, being the elder son, inherited the farms in Foxton when his father died in 1791, whereas Allen went to live in the nearby village of Orwell. Both sons married within a few years of each other. As already mentioned, William married Martha Sanxter in 1796 while Allen married Rebecca Pottrell on the 13 June 1793 in Chrishall, Essex.

William Stacey and Martha had five children by 1807. Over this time, and while they were growing up William and family in Foxton lived during the French Revolution and its aftermath. Following the Reign of Terror in France and the creation of the Directory in 1795, Napoleon Bonaparte became First Consul in a coup d'etat in 1799. Napoleon's expansionary aims in Europe caused Britain from then on to be at war with France on and off until 1815 when Napoleon was finally defeated at the battle of Waterloo. From Britain's point of view probably the most memorable event, apart from Waterloo, was the battle of Trafalgar in 1805 which established Britain's naval supremacy for the next hundred years and more. How much of these momentous events affected the lives of the Hurrells and their neighbours is perhaps best expressed by Rowland Parker in *The Common Stream*:

> *Search the records and what do we find? That Colonel Stewart reviewed the Basingbourne Militia on Foxton Common one day in 1804, and that Mr Hurrell afterwards provided refreshments, a memorable occasion which was 'graced by the presence of a great*

Chapter 7

part of the beauty of the district'. And that, so far as I can discover, was the only disturbance which the Napoleonic Wars inflicted on the tranquil life of the village. [That Mr Hurrell was William Stacey Hurrell]

Foxton House in 2007.

The Enclosure of the open fields of England had been proceeding since about 1760 and in the first 30 years of the 19th century this process caught up with Foxton.

William Stacey Hurrell and Bendyshe were the chief instigators of the Parliamentary Bill for the Enclosure of the open fields in Foxton parish in 1826, which dealt with 1,556 acres of open fields and common land and 137 acres of old inclosures.

When the Award was proclaimed in 1830 William was allotted 25 acres of closes and 350 acres of open fields to the west of the village where he had built his own house, Foxton House, by 1828, though it is not clear whether he occupied it immediately. By 1839, William's holding had grown to 385 acres.

Before we go on with the descendants of Allen – our descendants – we should continue the story of William Stacey's family. The first child, Ann, who was baptised on 8 January 1797, married Charles William Martindale, her first cousin, on 7 March 1829 and had four children by 1839. Ann died at the age of 45 years on 22 September 1842. Charles lived in and around Cambridge until 1871. The second child, William, was born before 1800 and was baptised at the same time as his sister Elizabeth on 2 November 1800. William died in 1856. The third child, Elizabeth, was born on 17 September 1800 and lived until 11 December 1886. Neither William nor Elizabeth married and had children. The fourth child, Allen, was born between October and November 1803; he married Theodosia Cavendish on 12 August 1825 in unusual circumstances in All Saints Church in West Bromwich, Warwickshire (see below). They had nine children, two of whom died young. The last child, Mary, baptised 19 April 1807 married Edmund Metcalfe, a surgeon, on 9 June 1846 in Melbourn, Cambridgeshire. Mary too died young and childless in May 1853 in Melbourn. Edmund married again and had five children.

William Stacey must have been disappointed not to have a son to continue farming. William was sickly and Allen was not interested and one gets the impression he was not reliable. The circumstances of his marriage in 1825 caused Allen to be out of favour with his father. The following excerpt from the *Cheltenham Journal* tells the story. At the time of the marriage Allen gave his address as Foxton Hall.

> *Leamington has been thrown into an uproar by the following occurrence:- William Allen Hurrell, son of William Hurrell, Esq., of Foxton-hall, Cambridgeshire, became some time since the favourite admirer of Miss Theodosia Cavendish, the protegée of Lady Musgrave, then a visitor at that fashionable watering place. The attentions of the young gentleman did not escape the notice of her ladyship, and she wrote to apprise his father of the acquaintance. The match did not meet the wishes of his parent, and a denial was the result. The young gentleman was in consequence told his visits would no longer be permitted, and the lady became more strictly watched. But love is ever fruitful in device; and opposition, it is well known, when directed against the stronger passions of our nature, only increases desire, and sharpens ingenuity. The youthful pair contrived to keep up a correspondence, and on Thursday evening, while the family of Lady Musgrave were at the assembly, the young lady having been previously locked up in her apartment, the ardent lover contrived to introduce himself into the house, broke out a panel from the door of*

Chapter 7

the chamber in which the fair captive was confined, and brought her forth in secret triumph through the aperture he had thus made. The hero of the story had arranged his plans well. A chaise was in readiness to receive the fugitives, and without a moment's delay they made their escape, and were married on the following morning at West Bromwich. This conclusion of the affair seems to have been apprehended by the friends of the young gentleman, as his uncle set off post, to prevent the anticipated match from taking place, but arrived six hours too late to effect his purpose. The happy bridegroom is of very respectable family, and the lovely bride is of high descent.

William Stacey signed his will on 5 February 1834, which reveals that he had tried to get Allen interested in farming by giving him the stock and crop on the farm when he admitted him to the farm as a yearly tenant. However, as events turned out Allen did not stay. William Stacey made his wife, Martha, his two daughters, Elizabeth and Mary, and his brother Swann his Executors, leaving out his son Allen. Moreover the will makes clear that his son William was not capable of looking after himself. At the Executor's discretion, the farm and all the estates were to be sold and the proceeds divided into six shares one of which was to be given to Martha and Swann Hurrell *'for the maintenance and support and providing all necessary comforts for my son William Hurrell'*. When Swann Hurrell died on 2 April 1834, Richard Cornings replaced him as Executor by Codicil. William Stacey died on 20 January 1836 and the will was proved on 21 October 1836.

In 1838, there was further trouble with Allen. It appears the Executors of the will had intended to withhold Allen's share of his father's will. Allen's wife, Theodosia, and children, and the Executors were the Defendants in a case brought by Allen to recover his inheritance. The reason given for withholding his share was that he had made a prenuptial pledge to settle upon Theodosia one half of whatever property he possessed thereafter and apparently he had reneged on that. The judge, however, ruled in Allen's favour that he was entitled to his share.

It was Allen and Theodosia's fifth child, Maria Elizabeth, who was the Major's *'one Mrs Nash of Royston (who) was a Miss Hurrell and was engaged to my Father but the family made them break it off as they were considered too poor'*. William

Hurrell, the Major's father, was Maria's first cousin once removed. Perhaps it was not so much that Maria's family was too poor but that her father, Allen, was persona non-grata with William's family owing to what they would have perceived as his unreliable nature. Maria eventually married Arthur Nash of Royston in 1863.

According to *British History Online*, the Hurrell's own farm, as distinct from Foxton Bury, was leased after the death of William Stacey but was not sold until 1856 after son William had died. No doubt William was cared for by the family during this period.

The Malting House, Foxton.

Martha and her daughter Elizabeth continued to live in Foxton for a time. At the time of the 1841 census they were living in the Malting House at the west end of the village together with five-year-old granddaughter, Elizabeth Martindale. James and Naomi Garner were residing at the Bury farm at that time. When Martha died in 1844 her will left £1,000 in trust to her Executors (about the equivalent of £52,000 today) to invest to pay the interest and dividends to her son Allen for his life, and after to his children. Then she left all her real estate and the rest of her goods, chattels, monies and personal effects to her daughters, Elizabeth and Mary. She made Elizabeth and Mary and her good friend the Reverend William Metcalfe, Rector of Fowlmere, Cambridgeshire, her Executors. (Mary married the Reverend's son, Edmund, in 1846 in Melbourn.)

Chapter 7

The following notice appeared in *The Times* of Wednesday 14 May 1856:

> *Messrs Cockett and Nash beg to announce that they are favoured with instructions from the Devisees under the will of William Hurrell, Esq., deceased, to SELL by AUCTION, in lots, early in June (unless an acceptable offer be previously made for the whole, of which due notice will be given) the substantial FAMILY RESIDENCE, known as Foxton House, with its ornamentally wooded grounds, three excellent malting offices, farmhouse, two farm homestalls, and 400 acres of productive light turnip and corn land, in a high state of cultivation. Also the Rectorial Tithe Rent-charge of the parish of Foxton, commuted at £538 10s per annum, with 20 acres of arable and pasture land, held on lease from the Dean and Chapter of Ely. Particulars, with conditions of sale and plans of the estate, are preparing, and may shortly be had of Messrs Thurnall and Nash, solicitors, Royston; and of the auctioneers at Royston and Hitchin.*

The whole farm was bought by William Ward Asplen and his wife Mary; it remained in the Asplen family until it was sold in 1904 when it was broken up.

The Maltings, Foxton in 1910.

So ended the association of the Hurrells with Foxton after 250 years, if the likes of Annabel and the first Thomas are taken into account. In the end it was Elizabeth who was the strength in the family, who was for a time a landed proprietor, lived for a time in Newton and ended her days in London. We can also see that the Major had confused Foxton House with Foxton Hall or Bury. He said Foxton Hall was owned by his great grandfather William and the Asplens owned Foxton Hall when he was a boy and had extended an invitation to visit them. The Hurrells did not own Foxton Hall or Bury although they had lived at the latter for nearly 100 years. They owned Foxton House at the end and the Asplens had bought Foxton House not Foxton Hall.

The 1841 census gives us an opportunity to get a snapshot of Foxton village at the time. There was a total of 450 people in the village on census night, 6 June 1841, comprising 13 farmers, 72 agricultural labourers, 71 wives, 237 children, 10 servants, 1 schoolmaster, 1 maltster, 3 carriers, 5 shepherds, 2 gardeners, 4 carpenters, 1 sackweaver, 2 shoemakers, 1 blacksmith, 1 brewer, 2 publicans, 1 butcher, 2 dressmakers, 1 nurse, 1 tailor, 1 housekeeper, 5 independents and 13 others.

* * * * *

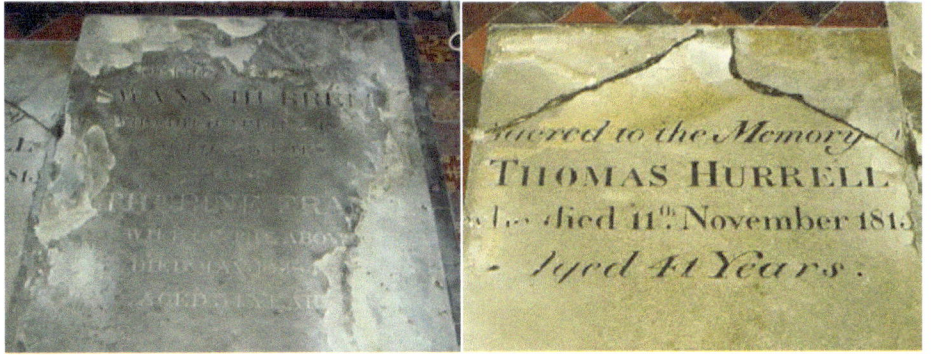

Hurrell floor plaques in the chancel of Foxton Church. Left, Swann Hurrell (died 1834) and his wife, Catherine Frances, née Finch (died 1846); right, Thomas Hurrell (died 1815), Swann Hurrell's brother.

Children of Allen Hurrell and Lucy Gordon

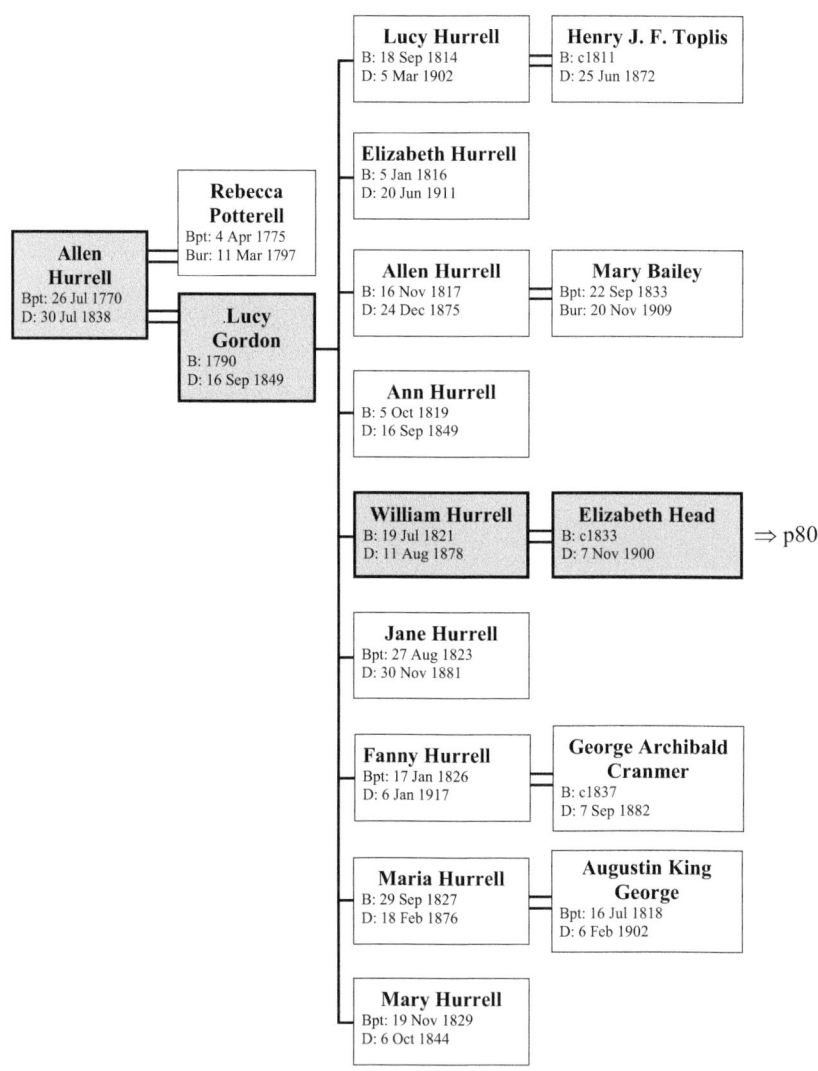

Chapter 8

Arkesden, Essex

Allen married his distant cousin Rebecca Pottrell on 13 June 1793, when he was aged about 25. Rebecca was baptised at Littlebury in Essex on 4 April 1775, so she may have been only 18 when she married. We know that Rebecca did not live long after the marriage, and no record has been found of any children. She was buried on 11 March 1797 in Chrishall, Essex. Rebecca's parents were John Pottrell and Jane Loveday. John died in 1778 or 1779 and was buried in Littlebury. He left a will which is of crucial significance to this history.

The last will and testament of John Pottrell, Gentleman of Littlebury Green, was signed on 25 November 1777 and said in reference to Rebecca '… *And all those my several messuages farms lands and hereditaments commonly called Peverells and Hobsary in*

Grave of Rebecca Hurrell (née Pottrell).

Chapter 8

Hobs Aerie farmhouse, Arkesden.

Arkesden aforesaid or in any other adjoining parishes with their rights members and appurtenances I give and devise unto my eldest daughter Rebecca and her heirs forever...' The farms and lands were charged with the payment of one annuity of £30 to be paid to his wife, Jane, for the term of her natural life. In her will signed on 21 January 1797 Rebecca left all her messuages, farms, lands and estates to her beloved husband, Allen Hurrell, and to his heirs and assigns forever. Thus, Allen came into possession of Hobsary, or Hobs Aerie (the Major's Hobbes Eyrie) in 1801 at probate of Rebecca's will.

Hobs Aerie is the name which is still in use today. Hobs Aerie and Peverells have always been linked and are in fact one continuous piece of land with Peverells, or what is left of it, lying adjacent to Arkesden village. *A Short Guide to the Parish of Arkesden, Essex* by J. B. Barnes, printed in 1967, lists four manors mentioned in the *Little Domesday Book** one of which is Hobs Aerie and Peverells. It is possible that the spelling 'Hobsary' is an ancient one. It was repeated in Allen Hurrell's will in 1838. The manor house, if there was one, was probably on Peverells. In 1855, among the documents in the Chancery case to be discussed later, there is the following passage:

> A freehold estate known as Hobs Aerie and Peverils situate at Arkesden in the County of Essex comprising Farm house outbuildings and 281 acres 3 roods 6 perches of arable pasture and wood land with the Manor or reputed manor of Peverils.

---

* *Essex, Suffolk and Norfolk were not covered in the main or Great Domesday Book survey in 1086, but were the subject of a survey published in the Little Domesday Book, shortly after the death of William I.*

The Major may have given the impression that Hobs Aerie was in the family for generations but the Hurrells owned Hobs Aerie for only 48 years as it was sold in September 1849.

Allen at Hobs Aerie was likely one of the instigators of the Parliamentary Bill for the Enclosure of the open fields in the parishes of Arkesden and Wendens Ambo in 1814. Commissioners and a land surveyor were appointed and after five years of work the Enclosure Award was made on 10 December 1819. Much of the southern part of Arkesden parish had already been enclosed with ancient closes and enclosed fields of arable lands. The open fields with their cultivated strips were mainly in the northern half where Hobs Aerie was situated. Thus in the proceedings of the Commissioners the parish was grouped as follows:

Ancient inclosed lands, grounds and homesteads	1268 acres
Open and common fields, common meadows, wastes and other grounds	1032 acres
Public and private roads and ways	10 acres
Town, streets and lanes	22 acres
	Total 2332 acres

At Hobs Aerie there were two ancient closes, one including Hobs Aerie homestead and Holme Close of 11 acres and the other at Peverells of 13 acres. In addition, there were about 10 acres of enclosed woods and 34 acres of enclosed arable lands before Enclosure. The Award allotted Allen much of the old open fields from Lower Field, Minchens Field, Bramble Bush Field and Plash Wood Field, thus making up his 282 acres. Most of Tows Field was allotted to the Vicar for tithes and this eventually became Arkesden Glebe.

Allen's second marriage was to Lucy Gordon in 1813 in St Mary's Church, Islington, Middlesex. This time Allen was aged 45 and Lucy was 23. Lucy was born in 1790 into a family of Cranmer Gordons, the first of eight siblings. Her father, Joseph Cranmer Gordon, a surgeon, by all accounts was the illegitimate son of Henry Cranmer of Quendon Hall, Quendon, Essex. Towards the end of his life, Henry was declared insane and after he died on 24 December 1810 a legal battle ensued in the Court of Chancery to determine his heir, the repercussions of which continued to 1834. Although Joseph was established as carer of his father and received some compensation he was not legally

Chapter 8

recognised as heir and lost claim to the farm and property, much to the chagrin of the family, (see Appendix 2).

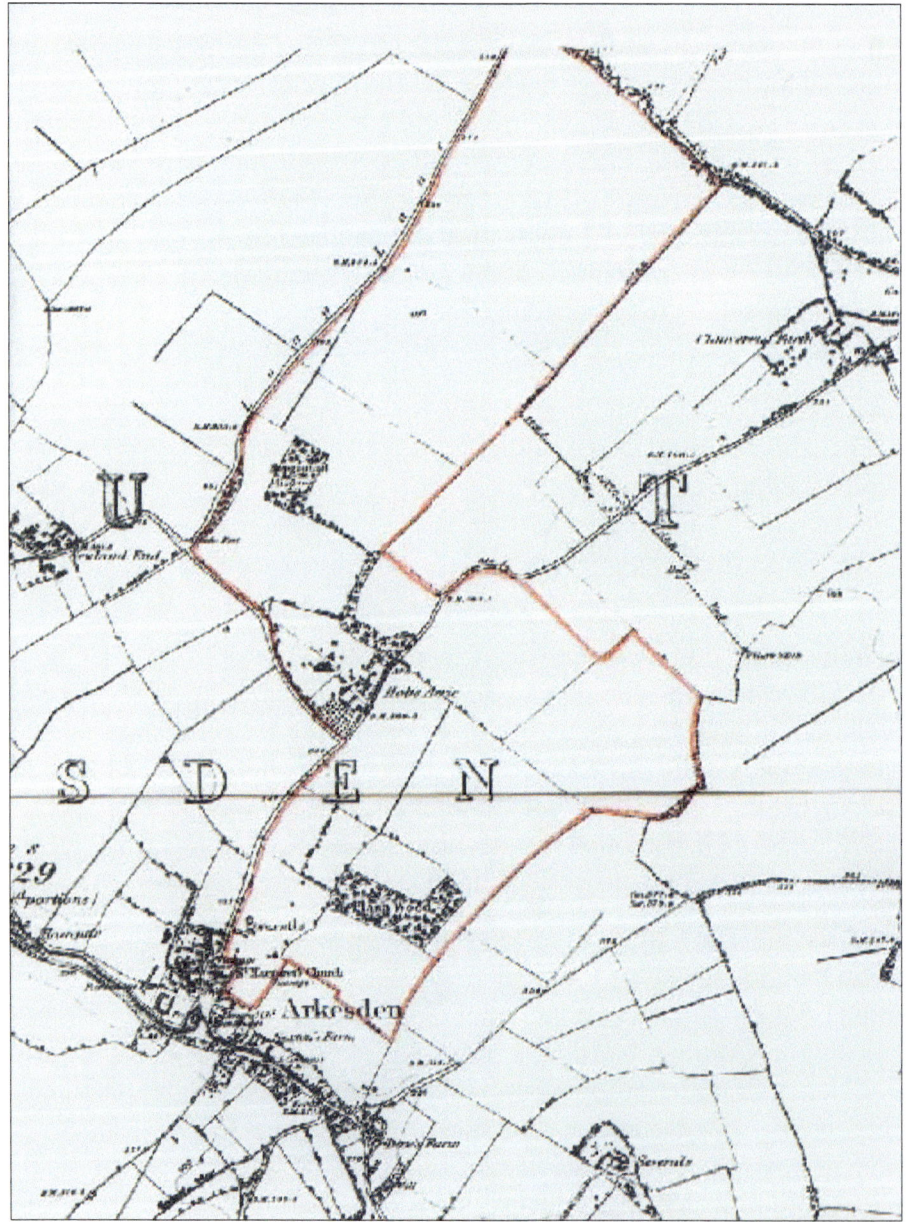

Hobs Aerie and Peverells farm boundaries in 1821.

Lucy's mother, also Lucy, died a widow on 6 January 1848 at 8 Frederick Street, Hampstead (probably Hampstead Road), the home of Henry Toplis who had become Lucy's son-in-law. The Reverend James Stewart Gordon Cranmer, who baptised the Major and his sisters in 1867, was Lucy's brother.

Allen and Lucy had nine children between 1814 and 1829 all born at Hobs Aerie, Arkesden. The first child born was Lucy on 18 September 1814. She married Henry John Fuller Toplis on 31 August 1841 at Arkesden. He was born about 1811 at St Pancras, London. At the time of his marriage, his brother owned the real estate business James Toplis & Son, 16 St Paul's Churchyard, London. Next was Elizabeth, born 5 January 1815, who lived to the age of 95 but remained unmarried. In some respects her life is similar to that of William Stacey's Elizabeth. Third was Allen, born on 16 November 1817. He married Mary Bailey on 12 August 1851 at the parish church, Wendon Lofts, Essex. At the time, Mary was a dairymaid at Clodmorehill, Arkesden; she was born in Elmdon, Essex, and was baptised 22 September 1833 in Arkesden. Her father was a farmer of 50 acres, employing two labourers, and running a beer shop at Elmdon. Allen and Mary had 11 children, three of whom died young at Arkesden.

Allen and Lucy's fourth child, Ann, was born 5 October 1819. Ann died in 1849 without marrying. William, the fifth child and father of the Major, was born 19 July 1821. There will be more to say about William later. Sixth was Jane born July 1823; she died in 1881 unmarried. Fanny was the seventh child born January 1826. She married her cousin, George Archibald Cranmer, on 29 January 1861 at St Saviour's Church, Maida Vale, London and had one child Ethel Annie Worthington Cranmer. George was a mate in the merchant naval service. He died on board the vessel Indus on 7 September 1882. Fanny was the last to die of all nine children, dying on 6 January 1917. The eighth child, Maria, was born 29 September 1827. She married Augustin King George on 2 April 1853 at St Georges Hanover Square, Middlesex. He was born 1 December 1817 in Enfield, Middlesex. He was a landed proprietor who lived at 43 Sussex Square, Brighton, in his retirement. They had seven children by 1869. Maria died in 1876 in Brighton but Augustin lived on to 1902.

The last child was Mary, baptised on 19 November 1829. She was only 14 years old when she died on 6 October 1844.

Chapter 8

Father Allen, mother Lucy, son Allen and his wife Mary, daughters Ann and Mary were all buried in the churchyard at Arkesden, as well as three children of Allen and Mary.

The last will and testament of Allen Hurrell of Arkesden, Essex, Gentleman, was signed on 14 January 1837. Unlike William Stacey, Allen's eldest son, Allen, wanted to continue farming so it is a mystery why he did not leave the farm to him but placed it in the hands of trustees, eventually to be sold, which led to untold difficulties further on. Two properties in Foxton were passed on to sons Allen and William – a one-acre allotment derived from the Foxton Enclosure Act to Allen and a freehold cottage or tenement *'with the yards Gardens Orchard and appurtenances thereto'* to William. (No doubt this is the property mentioned by the Major in his letter *'we owned a little land in the village still when I was a boy…the only reason for keeping it was a vote for Cambridgeshire'*.) The will then placed his whole estate, including farms Hobsary and Peverells and all other real estate, all household goods and furniture (except for those selected by his wife, Lucy, for her own use, up to a value of £200), farming stock, crops and implements of husbandry in the hands of his Executors, his cousin William Hurrell the younger of Newton, Esquire, Charles Rider of Littlebury, Essex, farmer, and John Cater Canning of Bishops Stortford, Hertfordshire, Gentleman; and he gave them full control of all the trusts and the authority to make all the decisions. John Cater Canning was the son of Thomas Canning, Vicar of Elsenham, first cousin of Lucy's sister Maria's husband, George Canning. As such, he was well known to the family and Allen probably considered him a reliable person for a trustee.

Further on in the will, as each child attained the age of 21 years, the trustees were to pay him or her £500 for their own absolute benefit. After Allen's decease, the trustees were to convert into money the whole of his residuary personal estate and invest the same and pay the dividends and annual proceeds, or so much of them as necessary, to his wife Lucy for the maintenance of herself and such of the children under the age of 21 years or, if a daughter, under that age and unmarried. Moreover, at their discretion, the Executors could continue farming and while the farms were carried on, the house at Hobs Aerie was to be kept as a residence for Lucy his wife during her widowhood and his children during their minorities. Finally, after the decease or remarriage of his wife or when all the children had reached the age of 21 years or, if daughters, that age or previous marriage, then the trustees were to sell the farm and all real estate and convert all his residuary personal estate, stocks and securities etc into money, and divide the total into 12 equal shares, the dividends and annual proceeds from which to be given to Lucy and the nine children with the two sons to receive two shares each. In addition to nominating the three named Executors, they and his wife, Lucy, were appointed as guardians of his children under the age of 21 years. Allen died on 30 July 1838 and the will was proved on 21 November 1838 in London. The terms of this will, together with the time during which the trustees held responsibility, set in turn a series of events that were to reshape and, to a degree, impoverish its beneficiaries, culminating in a ruling, some years later, by the Court of Chancery in London.

For a time after Allen's death the family stayed on in Hobs Aerie and farming continued, overseen by sons Allen and William. Payment of £500 a year was settled on Lucy, the mother, for the maintenance of herself and the children (£500 in 1838 would be worth about £27,000 today, enough for a comfortable living if supplemented with produce from the farm).

On census night, 6 June 1841, widow Lucy and her nine children were at Hobs Aerie. Their actual ages (those in the 1841 census are not precise) were daughter Lucy 26, Elizabeth 25, Allen 24, Ann 22, William 20, Jane 18, Fanny 15, Maria 13 and Mary 11. The census also revealed a total of 504 people in Arkesden parish comprising a further 10 farmers, 2 bailiffs, 70 agricultural labourers, 86 wives, 244 children, 27 servants, 8 widows of agricultural labourers, 1 carter's widow, 1 grocer, 3 carters, 1 shepherd, 1 gardener, 3 carpenters, 1 gamekeeper, 2 shoemakers, 2 blacksmiths, 1 harness maker, 1 publican, 1 thatcher, 1 draper, 1 clerk, 1 tailor, 13 independent and 12 others.

On 31 August 1841, the eldest daughter Lucy married Henry Toplis. A month later on 29 September (Michaelmas) the decision was made by the trustees to give up farming (the economic depression of 1840–1842 may have influenced their decision); the family moved out of Hobs Aerie and left Arkesden in October. The farm and house were leased to a Mr. Thurgood for £460 a year. The farm stock was auctioned: lots to the value of £275 1s 6d were purchased by son Allen. Crops and tillage were sold in two lots, one to Mr. Thurgood and one to Allen for £489 19s 6d. These purchases by Allen were not paid for

Chapter 8

Above: Arkesden Parish Church.

Left: A recent photograph of the Hurrell family altar tomb in the churchyard at Arkesden, mentioned in the Essex edition of The Buildings of England by Bettley and Pevsner (2007).

Arkesden

Modern Arkesden: The Church and road to Hobs Aerie [top left]; The Axe and Compass Inn and busy main street! [top and middle right]; The signpost on the Village Green [lower left]; View from the Green towards the Axe and Compass Inn [lower right].

Chapter 8

St. Mary the Virgin Church, Arkesden.

Becketts Farm, Arkesden.

and remained a charge against him until taken out of his entitlements. When the farming business was given up, it was arranged between the Executors and members of the family that, as Lucy Toplis was married and Allen Hurrell was living on his own (presumably at Becketts, a nearby farm hitherto managed by a bailiff), the sum paid to Mrs Hurrell should be reduced to £400.

The Hurrell family left Hobs Aerie at a time of significant social change in England. The first half of the 19th century was a time of unrest and protest. High prices combined with some bad harvests during the war years, from 1790 to 1815, made the period dismal for the poor. Rural areas as well as towns were the scene of repeated upheaval following the Napoleonic Wars, for example at Peterloo in 1819, the Captain Swing riots of 1830-31, culminating in Chartism and the revolutions of 1848. On the other hand, the coming of the railways after 1830 improved the transport of goods and people and the extension of schools and universities gathered pace after 1815.

The period was also the age of reform – reform of the franchise and repeal of the corn laws in particular. The Peterloo massacre occurred following a meeting of working people at St Peter's Field, Manchester, to demand the reform of Parliament as a step towards betterment of the people. Manchester was a case in point – it had a population of 200,000 but no Member of Parliament: ordinary people wanted government by the people for the people. A crowd of 50,000 to 60,000 caused the magistrates some concern and they called in the Yeomanry to control the crowd. Things got out of hand when the Yeomanry tried to arrest the speaker and a troop of hussars, trying to rescue the Yeomanry, caused a panic. In the succeeding melee, 11 people were killed and 400 injured.

In 1832, the Reform Act was passed by Parliament. The Act granted seats to large new cities and took away seats from the 'rotten boroughs' with very small populations. The Act increased the number of individuals entitled to vote to a total of about 653,000 adult males in a population of 14 million. The Act specifically disenfranchised women, sparking the British suffrage movement. The Act enlarged the county electorate. Owners of copyhold land worth £10 received the right to vote as did holders of long-term leases worth £10, holders of medium-term leases worth £50 and tenants paying an annual rent of £50. This did not satisfy all and further reforms occurred later.

The movement for political and social reform was continued in 1838 with the Peoples Charter which had six main aims: universal suffrage for men over 21 years: equal sized electoral districts: voting by secret ballot: an end to the need for a property qualification for Parliament: pay for members of Parliament and annual elections of Parliament. Chartism was mainly a working class movement as the middle classes had benefited by the Reform Act of 1832. Petitions were presented to the House of Commons in 1839 and 1842 but both were rejected by Parliament. There were several outbreaks of violence and there were strikes, arrests and trials. In 1848, after Karl Marx and Friedrich Engels had published the Communist Manifesto in London, a further large meeting of Chartists was held on Kennington Common and a further petition was presented to Parliament. This again came to nothing and the Chartist movement eventually petered out. However, in time, all of the Chartist's aims, except annual Parliaments, eventually came to pass.

On the economic front, the plight of agricultural labourers worsened after 1820 owing to several causes: loss of land rights as a result of the Enclosure movement, declining grain prices and an oversupply of labour resulting in a reduction in wages and the introduction of horse-powered threshing machines which could do the work of many men. A further grievance was the burden of the Church of England tithe system which had by this time been largely replaced by a cash levy which was often more than a poor person could afford. Rioting by impoverished and landless agricultural labourers commenced in 1830 with the destruction of threshing machines, workhouses, tithe barns and rick burning. The riots spread from the southern counties to the Home Counties (including Essex), the Midlands and East Anglia. Eventually the government dealt harshly with the rioters. Altogether nine of the rioters were hanged and a further 450 were transported to Australia. The riots were called Swing Riots because threatening letters, often signed by a 'Captain Swing', an unknown figure, were sent to magistrates, parsons and wealthy farmers. It is not known whether the Hurrells received any letters but once again most of these disruptions passed them by.

* * * * *

Chapter 9

The Chancery Case – Arkesden to London

After the family moved out of Hobs Aerie in 1841, family members dispersed to different places. The eldest child, Lucy, married to Henry Toplis, lived in London. Allen stayed in Arkesden at Becketts and the others probably found accommodation in London although we have no knowledge of where in London at this time. We do know from the Chancery papers that the others resided with and were maintained by mother Lucy until her death in September 1849 even after they had attained the age of 21 years. During this time, apart from Lucy and Allen, William was away for part of the time with Henry Toplis and the youngest, Mary, died in October 1844. The rent from the farm and returns on other investments in the terms of the will provided the income to support the family until the farm was sold in 1849.

The events that unfolded after 1841 reveal a gradually increasing concern and alarm as the family tried to ascertain its financial situation from the trustees in order to plan their future. At probate of the will it had been agreed that John Cater Canning would keep the accounts of the estate but when approaches to him drew a blank, appeals were made to William of Newton who showed little inclination to help. It should be remembered that William of Newton was a second cousin of the Arkesden children. Charles Rider, the third trustee was largely passive and inactive. Frustrated, the family finally issued a Bill of Complaint and the estate was put in the Court of Chancery in April 1850. The chronology of events outlined here is taken from the Bill of Complaint.

Dec 1843   Lucy Hurrell (mother) started writing to John Cater Canning (JCC) asking for the accounts. In January 1844, JCC promised to send them as soon as possible.

6 Oct 1844   Youngest daughter, Mary, died, aged 14 years 9 months.

April 1845   Lucy Hurrell (mother) wrote to JCC again… (we) *at present know nothing about our affairs and I think our expenses appear to be rather increasing instead of decreasing in consequence of so much illness.*

29 May 1845   Henry Toplis wrote to JCC about the accounts.

15 April 1846   Trustee William Hurrell married his first wife Ellen Seekamp.

25 Oct 1846   Henry Toplis wrote to trustee William Hurrell a long letter about the accounts… *You understand what (we want) to see is an account of all the monies received and paid by Mr Canning from the death of Mr Hurrell to the present time, the money having all passed through his hands; that account will show the precise position of affairs at this moment. These accounts he must of course have and one of Mr Taylor's Clerks could make a copy of them in two or three hours as well as in a month.*

In reply, trustee William Hurrell virtually rebuffed Henry Toplis but said… *My dear Sir, As an act of courtesy I am certain Mr Canning will give Mrs Hurrell the required information although I do not at all think he has at all laid himself open to the severe remarks your letter contained respecting the line of conduct pursued by him as Executor to the late Mr Hurrell… if any parties suffer it must be Rider and myself.*

1846 to 1848   Several other letters were written backwards and forwards about the accounts, but no accounts were produced. Details are in the Chancery papers.

June 1848	Cottage and blacksmiths shop, with freehold title under the will, was sold to William Hurrell for £160, but not paid for.
26 June 1848	James Toplis & Son, 16 St Paul's Churchyard, advertised the sale of Hobs Aerie Estate by Private Contract in The Times of London classifieds. (James Toplis was the brother of Henry.) The advertisement was repeated on 29 June 1848.
July 1848	Elizabeth (Betsy) and Ann went to stay with Allen (at Becketts, Arkesden) and saw JCC about the accounts to no avail.
11 Aug 1848	Lucy Hurrell (mother) wrote to JCC about the accounts once again… *It really is leaving us in such an unsettled state and inconvenience that I know not what to do. We have now only another month to remain in this house and I cannot inquire for another until I know what we shall have to live upon. I am very poorly and this uncertainty makes me quite ill.*
3 Sept 1848	Lucy Hurrell (mother) wrote to trustee William Hurrell about the accounts… *We must leave this house the end of this month and I have not been able to enquire for another being in total ignorance as to whether we should have anything to pay rent with or not… where are we to go?*
16 Sept 1848	William saw JCC about the accounts. He was told the accounts are in the hands of Mr Taylor, Solicitor to the trustees.
28 Sept 1848	Henry Toplis and William saw Mr Taylor at Stortford. Mr Taylor said he had not been instructed about the accounts.
29 Sept 1848	Maria, the youngest living child, turned 21.

According to the terms of the will, once the last child turned 21 the farm was to be sold, if not before, and the estate wound up. The farm was not sold until September 1849. As the last child was technically off her hands, the allowance for mother Lucy ceased. However, in view of the fact that there was no closure on the accounts, an advance was made to Lucy of £210. The worry, frustration and despair of mother Lucy and the family was only too evident in the letter Elizabeth (Betsy) sent to William of Newton, trustee, on the eve of their departure to France. We can only assume that, with so little to live on, France offered cheap accommodation. The address given, 8 Frederick Street,

Chapter 9

was the house belonging to Henry and Lucy Toplis where they presumably spent the last night before embarking:

> *8 Frederick Street, Wednesday October 4. My dear William, I am sorry to say that Mr Canning has not yet forwarded the accounts and we have very little hope that the means further to employed will induce him to do so and I think you will have the same opinion when I tell you that the first application of these accounts was made in 1844 when Mr Canning promised them without delay numerous applications have since been made and the excuses he had made for not sending them have been as numerous. At one time he was busy at his harvest, at another he was making important alterations in his will, at another his mother was seriously ill, at another Mr Taylor's clerks were merry making at Christmas (at that time 1844 it was supposed that they were in Mr Taylor's hands), in 1845 they were as nearly made out as possible but a document or two were mislaid and as soon as they were forthcoming they would be completed. In July last Anne and I went to Mr Canning to see about them ourselves he then promised them faithfully in less than a week. Not having heard from him another application was made and the following was the reply "August 14, with regard to the accounts they would have been ready some time ago, but that I was anxious that they should be made out without the expense of a lawyer and consequently I have worked at them myself and they would have been completed before now but for the last few days I have had friends which has prevented me finishing them etc" Not having heard any more of the matter William went down on the 16th of last month and saw Mr Canning who then told him that the accounts were in the hands of Mr Taylor who in moving from his old to his new offices had lost one document necessary to the completion of the accounts but that we should have them by the end of the week. Not having received them, Mr Toplis and William went to Stortford and saw Mr Taylor on Thursday last and enquired when we should have the accounts and if he had found the lost document. In reply he said he had never received any instructions to make up the accounts, he never received any documents relating to them therefore he could have lost none and that in fact he knew nothing whatever of the matter. I fear I have tried you with this long note, but we thought*

it better you should know before we left England. We gave up our house yesterday and go on board to night as the boat leaves at 4 o'clock in the morning. I hope we shall have a smooth passage as we are none of us very good sailors. I think you can sympathize with us in that feeling. We were pleased to hear from Melbourne (sic) that Mr Hurrell was much better, will you give our love to Eliza and with united remembrances to Mrs Hurrell and the remainder of your circle. Believe me My dear William Yours very sincerely Elizabeth Hurrell. P.S. If you have anything to write to us about will you direct to Lucy's and she will forward it to us.

As we shall see, they went to live in Boulogne. The Eliza mentioned in the letter was William of Newton's sister and his brother, Henry, was the Hurrell who later owned Madingley Hall. William of Newton himself was shortly to take over Manor Farm of 331 acres from his father so now the contrast in circumstances between the two sides of the Hurrell family could not have been more stark. It seems mother Lucy took with her to France Elizabeth, Ann, Jane, Fanny and Maria. Meanwhile on 28 October 1848, John Cater Canning got married, which event no doubt he used to procrastinate further on the accounts. He did finally produce a passbook in March 1849 which was considered totally inadequate by the family.

Just under a year after they reached France, on 16 September 1849, mother Lucy and daughter Ann died in Boulogne-sur-Mer after a short illness. The death certificate discloses they were living at Rue Neuve Chaussee with Monsieur Leroy, marchand de volailles, i.e. a poulterer. The certificate does not give the cause of death but it is highly likely it was cholera. Cholera reached Europe from India for the first time in 1832 with outbreaks in London and Paris which left many thousands dead. There was a second major epidemic in 1849 in several centres in France and England (particularly severe in London). The 'short illness' fits the description well as cholera is one of the most rapidly fatal illnesses known.

We do not know when the girls returned to England but two men came over to bring the bodies back to Arkesden where they were buried in the churchyard on 22 September. Mother Lucy was declared intestate and insolvent, 'indebted to certain tradesmen in several small sums'.

Chapter 9

It was six weeks before the family could once again focus on the fate of their inheritance. A further fruitless meeting was held on 3 November at the office of Taylor & Fairman of Bishops Stortford, Solicitors to the trustees, at which William of Newton, John Cater Canning, Henry Toplis and Allen Hurrell were present. The deficiencies in the passbook account were not explained. Thus, on 10 December 1849 Taylor & Collisson, Solicitors to the family, wrote to each of the trustees formally requesting a statement of receipts and payments relating to the accounts. When no satisfactory accounts were produced a Bill of Complaint was issued on 18 April 1850 and the estate was put in Chancery.

There followed due process which extended to 1856. The case was titled Toplis v Hurrell as daughter Lucy was the eldest in the family and she was married to Henry Toplis. Henry had been very helpful and active on behalf of the family since his marriage and he continued to do so during the long-running case. His help extended to making his house in London available to the family at different times. At the census on 30 March 1851 William was staying with his brother-in-law at 8 Frederick Street, St Pancras, Middlesex. Henry was described as a brewer employing two men and William's occupation was given as a Brewer's Collector, unmarried. Lucy Toplis was staying with her father-in-law, James Toplis senior, in Bloomsbury, London. James was a retired surveyor. Elizabeth, Jane, Fanny and Maria were at 13 Salisbury Place, Marylebone, in London, staying with Henry Browne, General Practitioner in medicine; they were all unmarried annuitants (presumably arising from the £500 each received when they reached the age of 21 years). Henry Browne either knew or knew of the family, as staying with him was his sister Ann Wright, and two visitors, Henry and Frances Prater, all three born in Arkesden, Essex. Allen was at Becketts, Arkesden, farming 250 acres. He married Mary Bailey on 12 August 1851.

A probable distraction from their worries for all of them at this time was the Great Exhibition held in Hyde Park, London, from 1 May to 15 October 1851. A special building named the Crystal Palace, a massive glass house, was constructed to hold the exhibits. Promoted by Prince Albert and opened by Queen Victoria, it was visited by six million people and was deemed a great success. It was designed to show off Britain's industrial technology and design.

William was still at 8 Frederick Street in 1852 when he wrote the following letter asking for a position in the Post Office:

> 8 Frederick Street
> Hampstead Road
>
> *My Lord*
>
> *I trust your Lordship will excuse the liberty, which I am fully sensible I am taking, in mentioning to address your Lordship. Although a stranger to your Lordship, the name of Hurrell is not entirely unknown in Cambridgeshire and Essex, in each of which counties, I have a small freehold, the one at Foxton near Cambridge, the other at Arkesden near Newport, & where I have had an opportunity, I have always been a firm supporter of the conservative cause. I am now thirty years of age, seven of which I have been in my present employment, which from circumstances I must shortly leave but with the best recommendation from the parties. If there should be a vacancy in the Post Office or any other public office I should ever feel grateful if your Lordship would use his influence to procure me the appointment.*
>
> *I have the honor to be,*
> *Your Lordships most*
> *Obedt, & humble servant*
>
> *William Hurrell*
>
> *30 June 1852*

The employment which William had been in for seven years must have been his apprenticeship as a brewer's assistant. The circumstances in which he had to shortly leave possibly refers to the necessity of his having to leave his brother-in-law's house.

The reply he received from the Post Office on 3 July enquired as to which member of the family he was, adding that his Lordship had already appointed one of his relations. William replied:

Chapter 9

> 8 Frederick Street
> Hampstead Road
>
> 5th July 1852
>
> Sir
>
> I beg to inform you, in reply to your letter of the 3rd Inst, that I am the younger son of the late Allen Hurrell of Arkesden, near Newport, Essex where my brother is now residing. I was not aware that any relation of mine was in the Post Office, but I presume it must be, either my cousin Allen Hurrell, late of Foxton, or one of his sons, with neither of which I have been in communication for some time past – to any other member of the family I can refer his Lordship.
>
> I am Sir
> Your obedt Servt
>
> William Hurrell

The reply he received on 18 September 1852 stated he was appointed a Clerk at Newport, Monmouthshire. Unfortunately we do not know if he took up the appointment but it is possible he did until the settlement of the Chancery case. It is hard to imagine how William could have tolerated for long the job of a Post Office Clerk.

The remainder of 1850 was occupied with the hearings of the joint and several answers of the Defendants William Hurrell, Charles Rider, and John Cater Canning to the Plaintiff's Bill of Complaint. The answers to the complaints continued through 1851 when points arising were submitted to the Master's Offices for investigation and report back. The hearings continued in 1852 and 1853 during which interrogatories were prepared by the Plaintiffs for the examination of John Cater Canning. On 2 April 1853, Maria married Augustin King George who thus joined the ranks of the Plaintiffs.

As part of this process, depositions, or answers to the interrogatories, were taken from John Cater Canning, 3 July 1854; Wyatt Given Gibson a partner in Gibson & Co, 3 July 1854; John Dobede Taylor, solicitor, 13 Jan 1855 and

3 Feb 1855; Elizabeth Hurrell, 10 Feb 1855; Jane Hurrell, 3 March 1855; Fanny Hurrell, 23 Feb 1855; Lucy Toplis, 23 Feb 1855; Allen Hurrell, 1 March 1855; William Hurrell, Plaintiff, 12 March 1855; Charles Rider, 16 April 1855; William Hurrell, Defendant, 13 April 1855 and Joseph Francis, 23 May 1855, bailiff of the farm after the death of Allen Hurrell. In addition, further voluntary statements made on oath known as affidavits were submitted to the Masters.

At the court hearing of the Master's Reports on 27 July 1854, the Plaintiffs and Defendants were represented by their solicitors except for John Cater Canning who did not attend although duly summoned. From here on John Cater Canning did not attend any further hearings. Whether he went to France, as the Major said, is not recorded.

The final Master's Report was heard on 15 November 1855 which summarised the situation arising from the previous hearings:

1) The ages of the children at their father's death and dates when they attained 21 were listed. It was noted that the daughter, Ann Hurrell died on 16 September 1849 having attained the age of 21 years but without having married and the Plaintiff William Hurrell was made the legal personal representative of Ann.

2) The receipts and disbursement of the Defendants were summarised. Receipts totalled £18308-13-9, amounts paid out £15229-10-5 leaving a balance due from the Defendants of £3079-3-4, which was not accounted for. It was acknowledged that the Defendants had already paid the sum of £2018-18-2 into the Bank with the privity of the Accountant General. Over the years the amount of £4601-13-4 paid to Lucy the mother was considered proper and necessary for the purposes of maintenance of the widow and children and education of the children.

3) No debt of the Testator was left unpaid. Advertisements were inserted in *The London Gazette*, *The Times* and the *Morning Chronicle* newspapers of 3 December 1852, the *Essex Herald* of 7 December 1852 and the *Chelmsford Chronicle* of 10 December 1852 requesting creditors to come in and prove their debts but no person came in.

Chapter 9

4) The funeral expenses of the Testator were paid and allowed the Defendants in the account of personal estate.

5) The legacies given by the Testator were paid and allowed the Defendants in the accounts.

6) No personal estate of the Testator was outstanding or undisposed of.

7) In the final analysis, the following moneys constituted the Testator's Residuary real estate which could be considered for distribution

The aforesaid amount paid into Court to the credit of this Cause	£2018-18-2
The aforesaid balance due from the Defendants	£3079-3-4
The balance due from the Defendants on account of rents and profits hereinafter mentioned	£117-3-8
Total	£5215-5-2

8) Sale of Hobs Aerie and Peverils at Arkesden in the County of Essex comprising Farm house, outbuildings and 281a 3r 6p of arable pasture and woodland with the Manor or reputed manor of Peverils, also a freehold Blacksmith's shop and cottage residence and garden at Arkesden realised the amount of £9533-14-0. This amount was paid out or allowed the Defendants, leaving no balance due.

Sale of Cottage	£160- 0- 0
Sale of rest of real estate	£9000- 0- 0
Timber	£338-11-0
Interest on purchase money and Inventory Stamps	£35- 3- 0
Total	£9533-14-0

9) The Defendants received rents and profits from the produce of the Testator's farm carried on from the day of the Testator's death to

Michaelsmas 1841 to the amount of £7505-14-8, and they paid or were allowed on account sums to the amount of £7388-11-0 leaving a balance due from them of £117-3-8 (see above).

10) The court found that the several payments made by the Defendant John Cater Canning were not made with the knowledge sanction or acquiescence of the Plaintiffs or any or either of them.

On 11 February 1856 the case entered the third and last stage of Decrees and Orders. It was ordered that the causes be transferred from the Book of Causes of the Right Honourable the Master of the Rolls to that of the Right Honourable the Lords Justices. At this meeting no one appeared for John Cater Canning.

On 8 May 1856 the following was resolved:

> *Upon motion made by Mr Roupell and Mr Bagally of Counsel for the Plaintiffs and upon hearing Mr Roundell Palmer and Mr Smith of Counsel for the Defendant William Hurrell and Mr Cairns and Mr Field of Counsel for the Defendant Charles Rider, this court doth order that each of the Defendants William Hurrell and Charles Rider do on or before the 9th day of June 1856 pay the sum of £500 into the Bank with the privity of the Accountant General of this Court subject to the further order of this court.*

On 12 June 1856 the final judgement was reached before the Right Honorable the Lords Justices in the presence of Counsel for all parties except the Defendant John Cater Canning for whom no one appeared although notice of the hearing had been duly served on him.

Upon confirmation of the payment into Court by the Defendants Charles Rider and William Hurrell of £500 each, the Plaintiffs consented to accept such payments in full discharge of all claims made against them. It was ordered that all further proceedings against the Defendants William Hurrell and Charles Rider be stayed.

It was ordered that the Defendant John Cater Canning on or before 15 July 1856, or within 7 days after service of the Order upon him, pay into the Bank with the privity of the Accountant General the sum of £2982-14-3 being the residue of the two sums of £3079-3-4 and £117-3-8 mentioned on 15 November 1855 as due from the Defendants with interest at the rate of 4% per annum from 18 April 1850 to date (*approx 6 years and 2 months*) less the two sums of £500 paid by the Defendants William Hurrell and Charles Rider.

After ordering the Defendants to forthwith execute a proper conveyance of the freehold blacksmith's shop and cottage residence at Arkesden to the Plaintiffs Allen and William Hurrell and arranging for the legal costs, expenses and legacy duties to be paid out of the sale of bank annuities and cash at the bank, the Lords Justices ordered the following sums to be paid out of the £4200 left available for distribution. It was recognised that the children had received differing amounts on account of their respective shares in the past and there was the need to distribute the remaining share to which Lucy the mother was entitled, and the Plaintiffs Lucy Toplis and Maria George having consented that their respective shares may be paid to their husbands the shares were apportioned as follows:

Henry John Fuller Toplis (for Lucy)	458-7-10
Elizabeth Hurrell	458-7-10
Allen Hurrell	589-8-00
William Hurrell (representing Ann Hurrell deceased)	708-8-10
William Hurrell	610-4-00
Jane Hurrell	458-7-10
Fanny Hurrell	458-7-10
Augustin King George (for Maria)	458-7-10
Total	£4200-0-00

The Justices insisted that this order was without prejudice to the rights of the Defendants William Hurrell and Charles Rider to recover from the Defendant John Cater Canning the sums of £500 so paid by them and their costs of this suit.

Under these terms William did well out of the settlement, perhaps by agreement of the others. He received £1318-12-10, which in today's money would be approximately £64,000. It was not a fortune but it probably enabled him to start up his business as a beer seller. The Major in his letter was perhaps quoting the settlement in terms of the value of the pound in the 1930s.

So ended the Chancery case. The whole episode, which had taken 18 years from the death of father Allen in 1838, resulted in the premature deaths of mother Lucy and Ann and caused a lot of unnecessary anxiety and disruption. John Cater Canning was the culprit but the Justices recognised that the other trustees were complicit in their failure to take action. Small wonder that the two branches of the Hurrells, in the words of the Major, never met again. There is, however, a sequel to this episode. In 1979 Geoffrey Dearsley Hurrell, on a visit to England, a descendant of the Plaintiff William, sat with Geoffrey Taylor Hurrell, a descendant of Henry the brother of Defendant William of Newton, outside Park House, Harston. The wheel had turned full cycle.

Geoffrey Taylor Hurrell and Geoffrey Dearsley Hurrell in Harston in 1979.

After settlement was reached in the Chancery case the Plaintiffs dispersed and resumed their lives. The eldest of the Hobs Aerie children, Lucy, married to Henry Toplis, settled in London, and for much of the time lived in Southampton Terrace, St Pancras, and later in Southampton Road. These places were not far from College Place, Camden Town, where William lived, so his Aunt Lucy would have been familiar to the Major growing up in the sixties and seventies. Lucy and Henry had no children. Henry died in 1872 at the age of 61 but Lucy lived to 87, dying in 1902.

The next of the Hobs Aerie children, Elizabeth, never married but also lived to a great age, dying in 1911 at the age of 95. For the last 30 years of her life she lived with her brother-in-law Augustin King George in Brighton, Sussex,

Chapter 9

after his wife, Maria, died in 1876. In the 1891 census it was recorded that Elizabeth was blind.

Meanwhile, over in Arkesden at Becketts, Allen and his wife Mary were raising a family. By 1856 they already had four children: Jane born 1852, Allen 1853, William 1855 and Catherine 1856. In 1859 tragedy struck at Becketts. William and Catherine died in September and October of that year at the ages of four and three. The cause of death in both cases was 'Cynanche Maligna'. This was an archaic term used to describe diphtheria, an infection of the throat with swelling and the formation of an abscess sometimes leading to choking and death. When the next child, Kate, born at the end of 1859 died in April 1861 at about 18 months old the cause of death was described specifically as diphtheria. Today, with the help of antibiotics, these children would probably have lived. The three little ones are buried in Arkesden churchyard.

Allen and Mary had another child at Becketts named William Bailey Hurrell born on 30 January 1861, who as an adult migrated to Australia and died in 1934 at the age of 73, in Orange, New South Wales. Not long after William Bailey's birth, in 1863, Allen and Mary gave up farming, perhaps because of the loss of their children. Another five children were born elsewhere at Stansted, Essex, and at Poplar, London, where they eventually settled. When Allen and Mary died they were buried in Arkesden churchyard with the three little ones (see Appendix 3).

Jane also never married. She lived her life mainly in London but in 1871 she was living in Hastings, Sussex. At the census of 1861 she was described as a fund holder and in 1871 she was a railway shareholder. She died at the age of 58 in 1881 and the cause of death was epileptic convulsions.

Fanny was also long lived. In January 1861, at the age of 27, she married her cousin George Archibald Cranmer, a mariner, a mate in the merchant service, aged 23. They lived mostly in London but after George died, Fanny moved to Brighton, Sussex. Fanny and George had one child, Ethel Annie Worthington Cranmer. George died on 7 September 1882, but Fanny lived on to 1917 aged 90. Fanny is buried in Kensal Green Cemetery, London. There is a memorial to her on the family tomb in the churchyard at Arkesden. She was the last surviving child of the Hobs Aerie family. After her mother died, Ethel continued to live in Brighton until her death in 1927 at the age of 62. Ethel left money in a trust fund at Arkesden to be used for the poor and the upkeep of the Hurrell graves:

THE HURRELL CRANMER EPIPHANY TRUST FUND 1917

Being the capital sum of Three Hundred Pounds given by Miss L. A. K. Cranmer in memory of her beloved Mother Mrs Fanny Cranmer daughter of the late Mr Allen Hurrell to the Vicar of Arkesden and two other Trustees who shall use the annual income of the Trust Fund for the benefit of the Poor who have been resident in the said Parish of Arkesden for at least one year, whilst and so long as the Trustees, out of the said annual income of the Trust Fund shall keep in general good repair and preservation the family tomb of the said Mr Allen Hurrell.
(Transcription of the above plaque in Arkesden Church.)

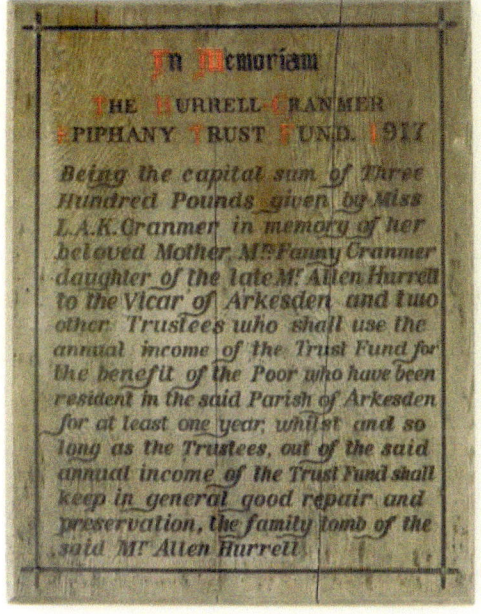

Three hundred pounds in 1917 would be worth about £8,700 today. Miss L. A. K. Cranmer was, in fact, Fanny's daughter, Ethel Ann Worthington Cranmer (see Appendix 3).

Maria, the youngest living child at the settlement in 1856, had married Augustin King George in 1853. They raised a family of seven children between 1854 and 1869, mostly born in Paddington, London. Two of their children died at an early age. By the time Maria died in 1876 they too were in Brighton, Sussex. Maria suffered from a general debility for six months followed by a sudden collapse. As already mentioned, Augustin lived on in Brighton and was joined by his sister-in-law, Elizabeth. He died in 1902, at the age of 84. Starting off as a landed proprietor and fund holder he ended his days living on his own means (see Appendix 3).

* * * * *

Children of William Hurrell and Elizabeth Head

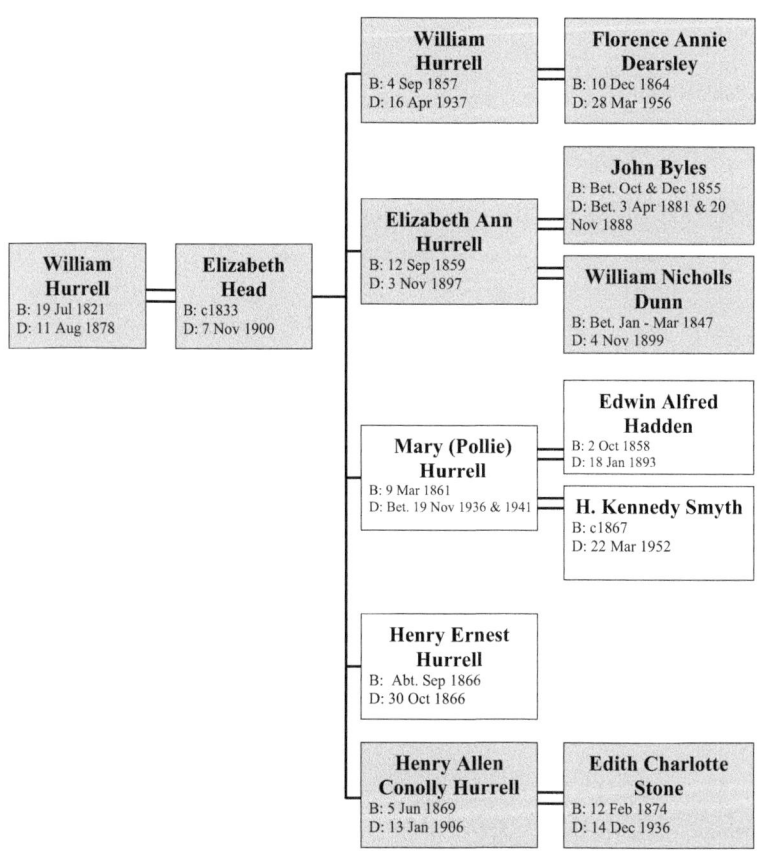

Chapter 10

London – Camden Town

Where William lived when he received his share of the settlement in 1856 is not known but a year later he was in London for the birth of his first child. That is if the census of 7 April 1861 is to be believed. On census night, William, Elizabeth and son William (the Major), 3 years old, were at 21 College Place, St Pancras, Middlesex. Son William's birthplace was given as Camden Town, London. College Place is part of Camden Town. (The Major's birthday was in fact 4 September 1857.) Along with son William aged 3, there was a daughter Elizabeth Ann aged 1 and an unnamed daughter aged one month. The latter was Mary. They also had a house servant, Mary Mackherry aged 15. Elizabeth Ann and Mary were also recorded as born in Camden Town although the census of 1871 and her registration certificate revealed that Elizabeth Ann was actually born in Dover. Father William's occupation was given as 'beer seller', which meant he was entitled to sell beer from home. Mother Elizabeth's birthplace was recorded as Berkshire.

There was an element of mystery surrounding the identity of William's wife, Elizabeth, their marriage and son William's birth. Son William's birth was never registered, or if registered has never been found, although the births of all the other children were registered. It is known that about ten per cent of births in England and Wales have not been registered over time. As to Elizabeth, her identity was established by a roundabout route. She recorded her maiden name as Head on the birth certificates of her children, Elizabeth Ann, Mary and Henry (and later, on her marriage certificate). At the census of 1871 Elizabeth gave her birthplace as Berkshire, Ilsley, and in later censuses as Berkshire, Wantage (Wantage being the registration district). Her age as recorded on the census returns gave a likely birth date of 1836, which is before the introduction of civil registration of births, deaths and marriages in England.

As it appeared that William's wife, Elizabeth, was born in Ilsley around 1836, a search was made of the census returns for Ilsley in 1841, which revealed a family of Heads in East Ilsley, Berkshire, with one child. Joseph and Honour Head had a 3-month-old child, Maria. Ten years later, at the 1851 census, Honour was alone in East Ilsley, a widow, described as a pauper, with two children, Maria and Emma. In between these events Joseph and Honour had a third child Mary Ann who was born in 1845 and died in 1849. Joseph also died in 1849 and was buried on 28 August in East Ilsley. Joseph's occupation was described at different times as servant, post boy, agricultural labourer and grocer. Although Elizabeth was not present in East Ilsley in 1841 or 1851 her relationship to Honour was eventually established through Maria Head who grew up to marry Charles Stanton and went to live in Williamscote, Oxfordshire. They had a daughter Florence Mary and on the night of the 1891 census, when Elizabeth was in charge of the pub 'George and Dragon' in Wandsworth, 15-year-old Florrie Stanton, born in Williamscote, was staying at the pub and was recorded as Elizabeth's niece. The whereabouts of Elizabeth's birthplace however remained a mystery until an entry in the Wanborough Parish Records, in Wiltshire, finally provided a clue.

The Wanborough Parish Records show Elizabeth's mother, Honour Head was born Honor (*sic*) Wayte in Wanborough, Wiltshire, in 1808, one of eight children of William and Hannah Wayte. She was baptised on 12 June in Wanborough. On different documents their name was variously spelt Wait, Waite, Wayte and even White. William Wayte was a labourer. Honor's sister, Sarah, was baptised on 19 May 1811 and in the 1830s Honor and Sarah gave birth to several children whose baptisms were recorded in the Wanborough Parish Registers:

Mary	4 November	1832	(daughter of Sarah)
Mary Agnes	26 May	1833	(daughter of Sarah)
Elizabeth	15 December	1833	(daughter of Honor)
Emma	14 September	1834	(daughter of Sarah)

All four children were recorded as base born which means they were born of a single mother. The first Mary died and was buried on 6 January 1833 (hers was obviously a late baptism). Elizabeth was baptised twice, having been first recorded in the Wantage Parish Register on 28 October 1833 (mother Honor Waite, single woman) and later as above. After her mother married Joseph Head on 19 October 1840 Elizabeth must have assumed the name of Head at some stage but not before the census of 1841 when she was staying in Wanborough with her grandmother, 70-year-old Hannah White. She was listed as Elizabeth White aged 8 along with her aunt Sarah and cousin Emma aged 7. At the 1851 census her 17-year-old cousin Emma Wait was staying with the family of Simeon James Etty, the Vicar of Wanborough, as a house servant. However, 18-year-old Elizabeth's whereabouts in 1851 are not known. So when Elizabeth gave her birthplace on later censuses as Berkshire, Wantage, it was at least the place of her first baptism and may have been the actual place of her birth. One might ask how it came to pass that Elizabeth Head from Berkshire met William Hurrell in London. It is possible she came to London looking for work as many were doing at that time, and she took employment in William's beer selling business. Her mother, Honour, ended her days staying with her daughter Maria and family in Oxfordshire.

Returning to 21 College Place, after the birth of Elizabeth Ann on 12 September 1859 and Mary on 9 March 1861, a son Henry Ernest was born in September 1866. He died of convulsions one month later. The last child to be born was named Henry Allen Conolly Hurrell, born on 5 June 1869 in Camden Town like the others, except for Elizabeth Ann, who as previously stated was born in Dover. On the death certificate for Henry Ernest, the occupation of William the father was recorded as 'brewer'.

William and Elizabeth were in no hurry to baptise their children or formalise their relationship. Eventually, perhaps at the insistence of Elizabeth or urging

Chapter 10

25 October 1867 – Baptisms of William, Elizabeth and Mary Hurrell

London – Camden Town

1 February 1868 – Marriage of William Hurrell and Elizabeth Head

6 February 1870 – Baptism of Henry A. C. Hurrell

of family members such as William's sister Lucy Toplis, the first three children were baptised together on the 25 October 1867 at St John the Baptist Church, Clerkenwell, by J. Stewart Gordon Cranmer, Minister. Their address at the time was 21 College Place, Camden Town. William recorded 'Gentleman' as his trade or profession. The following year, on 1 February 1868, William Hurrell and Elizabeth Head were married in the Parish Church of St John, St Pancras, Middlesex. Their address at the time of marriage was given as 90 Charlotte Street. William's occupation was 'brewer', William's father was recorded as Allen Hurrell, Gentleman, and Elizabeth's father Joseph Head, Grocer. They were married by Francis Henry Dinnis, MA, and the witnesses were Lucy's husband, H. J. F. Toplis and Harriet Scott.

Eight months after Henry A. C. was born, he was baptised on 6 February 1870 in the Parish of Old St Pancras, Middlesex by G. Nicholls. Their abode was 21 College Place and William was again a 'brewer'.

Growing up in the sixties and seventies was in a time of rapid change; the population of England and Wales was moving rapidly from the country to the towns. In 1800, two-thirds of the population lived in the country in rural villages but, by 1871, the situation had reversed and two thirds of the population lived in towns, the majority in large towns. And there was none larger than London. Along with this migration the Industrial Revolution grew apace bringing with it a need for efficient transportation and ease of movement. The railway network which had started early in the 19th century had by 1854 established six railway terminals just outside the centre of London. Traffic congestion in the city led to the idea of building an underground railway to facilitate movement between the city and these terminals. Construction of the first underground railway, the Metropolitan Railway, between Paddington Station and Farringdon Street via Kings Cross, began in February 1860 and opened in January 1863. Thereafter, to the end of the century and beyond, more lines were constructed and the network gradually extended to cover the whole of London.

In 1867, Disraeli's Conservative Government introduced a new reform of the franchise. The 1867 Reform Act gave the vote to every male adult householder in a borough constituency, also male lodgers paying £10 for unfurnished rooms. This gave the vote to about 1,500,000 men. It was after this Act was passed that William and Allen probably sold their properties in Foxton and Arkesden, which were no longer needed to provide them with the right to vote.

Across the Atlantic, the American Civil War raged between 1861 and 1865. Britain remained a wary and distant observer of this first of the modern wars where frontal assaults were overwhelmed by massed firepower. It is certain that newspapers of this time would have been full of reports of the battles and campaigns; however, William and Elizabeth raising their family in London probably had more pressing problems, such as where to send the children to school.

In later life the Major said he went to the 'North Collegiate School'; this was undoubtedly the North London Collegiate School in Camden High Street. In 1850, the North London Collegiate School for Boys was founded to educate boys from middle class homes. It opened at 12 Camden High Street in 1852 while at the same time a school of the same name opened for girls in the same area. The North London Collegiate School for Girls continued on to the present day, gaining in prestige, whereas the boys' school closed in about 1897. The girls' school eventually moved away from Camden Town and is now located in the London borough of Harrow. From 1897, the boys' school building was used as a cabinet factory by the firm of house furnishers Oetzmann & Co. The building was demolished after 1955.

North London Collegiate School building after closure.

Chapter 10

In the early years after the school was opened there must have been a certain amount of hostility shown by local lads towards the 'young gentleman' at the school. A cautionary notice was posted by a local magistrate in 1857 warning against boys causing annoyance. William, the Major, probably attended the school in the late sixties and seventies. The school was only a short walk from where he lived in College Place. In 1868 a statue of Richard Cobden was erected in Camden High Street right outside the school.

Maintaining good order!

The unveiling of the statue of Richard Cobden MP in 1868 outside the North London Collegiate School in Camden.

A photograph of the unveiling on 27 June 1868 captured the scene of the large crowd gathered in the street. Richard Cobden was a Member of Parliament who had led the successful campaign for the repeal of the Corn Laws in 1846, which had removed the tariffs on imported corn. If William was at the school then, he would have only just started. The school is seen at the top right-hand corner of the photograph.

Undated photograph of boys at London School, possibly at 7 Highgate Road, St. Pancras.

A photograph (above) belonging to members of the family in Africa, taken sometime during this period, shows a group of 41 boys with a master and perhaps an assistant teacher which is thought to include William, although there is no confirmation of this and the photograph has never been dated. It has been suggested that the boy in the front row, third from left, may be William. We have no knowledge of where the girls went to school, whether or not they went to the North London Collegiate School for Girls. At the census of 1881, when Henry would have been 11 years old, only mother Elizabeth and daughter Mary were present at home. At that time William the father was dead, William the Major was in Africa and daughter Elizabeth Ann was married and living away. It is likely that the following entry from the 1881 census at a private school for boys is for Henry but at present no proof is available: *7 Highgate Road, St Pancras, Henry Hurrell aged 10 years, born London, Middlesex, Boarder.* The census lists 43 boys, all boarders. The ages range from 6 to 16, with 25 boys aged between 10 and 13. Camden Library has been unable to do more than confirm the existence of a private boys' school run by Mr. Harry Giles who continued to do so until at least 1888. Along with Harry Giles, aged 28, on census night were a matron, cook, housemaid and house boy. The school was already in existence at 7 Highgate Road ten years earlier in 1871 when Harry's grandmother, Sophia Giles, widow, aged 68 years, was the schoolmistress in charge and Harry, aged 18, and his sister, Emma, aged 19, were teachers. There were also a 'School Teacher General', cook, housemaid and assistant servant living in on census night together with 23 boys all boarders (William Hurrell was not one of them). Ten years before that on census night 1861, Sophia Giles was 'Principal of Boys School' at 9 and 10 Willow Walk, St Pancras, with Emma, aged 9, and Harry, aged 8. There were two schoolmasters, a wardrobe keeper, cook and manservant and 32 boys. Indeed, the photograph on the previous page of a group of boys is more likely to be a photograph of boys at Henry's school rather than William's. Having moved from Camden Town to Wandsworth, it was no longer possible for Henry to go daily to North London Collegiate. It is possible the photograph above was sent to William in South Africa by his mother sometime in the early 1880s.

In *The Oxford History of England: England 1870 – 1914*, Sir Robert Ensor gives the history of two depressions at this time. The first started in 1873 at Vienna and, by 1876, the slump had become general in England. For three years English industry suffered the brunt of the great depression while the agricultural depression went on steadily deepening after 1878. The second crisis started in 1882 in Paris and was succeeded by a continued fall in prices which lasted for three years. The main cause of these depressions was the invasion of Europe by wheat from the American prairies in the late seventies, brought about by the improvement in railways, steamships and agricultural machinery. The situation was exacerbated by bad wet summers from 1875 to 1879, an outbreak of rinderpest disease in 1877 and an epidemic of Foot and Mouth disease in 1883.

William the Major's decision to go out to South Africa in 1877 at the age of 20 may have been due solely to a sense of adventure but the lack of opportunity at home at this time must also have been a factor. At any rate, in that year he joined the Frontier Light Horse, a colonial force in South Africa and was almost immediately engaged in the Gaika and Zulu wars which we will come back to later.

* * * * *

William Hurrell of Wandsworth 1821–1878.

HURRELL William.

Personal Estate under £600.

4 October. The Will of William Hurrell formerly of Frederick-street Hampstead-road in the County of Middlesex Brewer but late of the "George and Dragon" Public House West Hill Wandsworth in the County of **Surrey** Licensed Victualler who died 11 August 1878 at the "George and Dragon" was proved at the **Principal Registry** by Elizabeth Hurrell of the "George and Dragon" Widow the Relict the sole Executrix.

Entry in the Wills and Probate Calendar for 1878.

Chapter 11

London – Wandsworth

Back home the Major's father, William, was nearing the end of his life. He must have prospered reasonably in his brewing business for Young's Brewery has advised that William took over the tenancy of the pub 'George and Dragon' in West Hill, Wandsworth, in February 1878 which was just six months before he died. Young's records show that Elizabeth was the tenant thereafter, succeeded by Henry when she died in 1900. The George and Dragon was closed for business on 31 December 1903 after which it was demolished to widen the road. In February 1904, Henry became tenant at 'Ye Olde Bull' in Wandsworth. William died on 11 August 1878, aged 57, and was buried in the Garrett Lane Old Burial Ground, Wandsworth. The cause of death was given as cirrhosis of the liver. Sometime, probably in the 1870s, William had his photo taken which later was mounted with a vignette in Alec Binnie's studio in Putney at the same time that Elizabeth had hers taken in the 1890s.

Elizabeth, ably assisted by barman George Ostler, continued to manage the pub for the next 22 years. Mary and Henry A. C. grew to adulthood in the environs of the pub. A picture probably taken before the turn of the century

Chapter 11

The George and Dragon in the late 1890s.

shows the busy street in which the pub stood. The sign 'George and Dragon' is visible hanging below the roof line in the middle of the picture above.

The second of the children to leave home was Elizabeth Ann. She married John Byles, a Railway Clerk, on 1 March 1878, at the age of 18, at St Matthew's Church, Oakley Square, St. Pancras (just after the move to Wandsworth). William, her father, was one of the witnesses. They had one child, Florence Annie Byles, born on 5 March 1879. The marriage seems to have been short lived. At the 1881 census, John Byles was a boarder with a family named Cole at 24G Street, Hans Town, Chelsea, while the whereabouts of Elizabeth Ann and Florence is not known. Harry Cole was a Railway Clerk and John was described as a Clerk, idle. John Byles died sometime before 1888 and Elizabeth Ann married again to William Nicholls Dunn on 20 November 1888 at St James Church, Fulham, Middlesex. The couple already had a child, Ethel Annie Dunn, born on 9 July 1887 at 41 Ashgrove, Wavertree, Liverpool, Lancashire. William Dunn was a Barrister's

Clerk. At the 1891 census, William Dunn, Elizabeth Ann and Ethel were living at 43 Waldemar Avenue, Fulham, Middlesex. At the same time, Florence Annie Byles, aged 12 years, was staying with her grandmother Elizabeth at the George and Dragon. Again, Elizabeth Ann's marriage was short lived because she died aged 38 years, on 3 November 1897, after 15 months of suffering from cancer of the uterus. At the time of her death she was living at 3 Lebanon Terrace, West Hill, Wandsworth, and she was buried in the Wandsworth Cemetery. William Dunn died two years later and he was buried in the same cemetery (see Appendix 3).

The third child, Mary, also known as Pollie, lived at the George and Dragon until she married Edwin Alfred Hadden at the age of 24 years on 18 November 1886 at St Mark's Church, Battersea, Surrey. Edwin progressed from being a Commercial Cook to a Hotel Proprietor eventually becoming the Licensed Victualler of the Imperial Hotel, Hastings, Sussex. It was here that Edwin and Mary were living on census night, 5 April 1891. The marriage was childless and Edwin died on 18 January 1893. Mary, seeking a change, went to Rhodesia (now Zimbabwe) to join the Major. There she met and married Henry Kennedy Smyth M.B. (Harry) on 15 November 1897 in Gwelo, Rhodesia. The marriage was performed by the Lord Bishop of Mashonaland. Pollie and

Mary (Pollie) Hurrell.

Harry were both musical and played the piano well. Again, the marriage was childless and the couple eventually moved to Cape Town. Mary died in George, South Africa, predeceasing Harry, who died on 22 March 1952. On his death notice, Mary's death is given as 1940-41. The above picture of Mary was taken in St Leonards-on-Sea when she was married to Edwin Hadden.

All this while William, the Major, was living a life of action in South Africa. When the British army invaded Zululand in 1879 it set off a series of dramatic actions in which the Frontier Light Horse was involved. The slaughter of the

Chapter 11

24th Regiment by the Zulus at Isandlwana and the subsequent heroic defence of Rorkes Drift, which have been portrayed in films, have overshadowed the action at Hlobane Mountain in which William took part, which was every bit as dramatic and dangerous. The following extract from a letter he wrote to his mother in Wandsworth dated 4 April 1879 was printed in *The Foreman Engineer and Draughtsman* of 1 June 1879 and gives a graphic account of that action.

> *My Dearest Mother - Before this letter reaches you will have heard the news of Colonel Wood's - "ours" - column having had two engagements with the Zulus, in the latter of which we killed and wounded about 6000 of them, and until you receive this letter I am certain you will feel uneasy about me, so I drop a few lines to let you know that I am still "alive and kicking." This fact, however, I can hardly believe myself, as on the 28th of March, out of about 400 mounted men that left our camp the day before, 97 were left dead, and only 8 were brought in.*
>
> *On the 27th March we left camp, about 400, all mounted, with rations for three days, intending to take Zlobanne Mountain, a very strong place indeed. We got close up to it under cover of darkness, and slept that night with our horses saddled and bridled ready in case of an attack, and at about 3 a.m. on the 28th, just before daybreak, we commenced to ascend the mountain. The enemy were evidently on the alert, for we had not got far when they opened fire on all sides. The first to fall was Lieutenant Williams, of our corps; he was shot dead through the head. Well we carried the mountain in splendid style, and, as we thought, thoroughly beat the Kaffirs; but whilst on the top, where we were still engaged with some of them, we saw thousands of others coming in all directions to reinforce those with whom we were fighting; so numerous were they that Colonel Buller ordered us to retreat at once. The only way to do this was by a very steep and bad pass, down which we had to lead our horses, whilst the Zulus kept up a heavy cross-fire on us. Many horses had to be left behind with broken limbs, and still more were shot. About threefourths of us had got clear of the pass, and some made a stand on a rise, and did our best to cover the retreat of those who were still*

coming down. Then hordes of Zulus arrived and fell upon our brave fellows, thus commencing a fearful slaughter of our comrades under our very eyes, and not 400 yards from us. A few still managed to get away by letting their horses go and running for dear life, but 90 odd fell and were shot and assegaied within range of us, and although we kept up a deadly fire all the time. Then again we had to fly to the bottom of the next hill, where we made another stand, and a few more were killed, and as they were fast getting round us we once more had to retire; but we had now reached the plain, and succeeded in making our way to the camp.

I lost several personal friends in this disastrous affair, and God knows how I myself got through it safely. One dear chum was wounded in the leg where we made the second stand. He got off his horse to look at the wound, and before he could mount again he was speared to death! I brought off another fellow all the way to camp, riding behind me on my horse, he, poor fellow, having been severely wounded in traversing the pass. All that were killed were volunteers

Many fellows were so panic-stricken that directly they got down the pass they bolted, and never drew rein until they reached the camp, a distance of 25 miles; those, however, who did thus were mostly recruits, and never before been under fire. I am to get promotion, which means another 1s per diem, and to be a non-commissioned officer, for sticking to the colonel and doing my best to cover the retreat of the others.

The letter goes on to give an account of the action the next day when the main force of the Zulus attacked the camp at Kambula and were killed in their thousands. William paid tribute to the bravery of the Zulus making repeated rushes on the camp to fall under the constant fire.

After the final defeat of the Zulus, William went prospecting for gold in what was then the Eastern Transvaal, now the province of Mpumalanga. During the 1880s he pegged claims in partnership with others at sites near Pilgrims Rest and Barberton, places and a time immortalised by Sir Percy Fitzpatrick in *Jock of the Bushveld*. In fact it is likely that he knew or knew of Fitzpatrick and

Chapter 11

Major William Hurrell and his wife, Florence (née Dearsley).

his dog. He must have done reasonably well for he was able to return to England in 1890 and married Florence Annie Dearsley on 10 January 1891 at St Saviours, Pimlico, London. At the 1891 census, 5 April, they were in London staying at 34 Hugh Street where William was 'living on own means'. Confusingly, on the census form, William recorded he was born in Arkesden, Essex. As no record of birth has ever been found for William, it is impossible to verify this claim. Apart from his uncle, Allen, all the Hurrells had left Hobs Aerie and Arkesden in 1841, 16 years before William was born. Hobs Aerie was sold in 1849 so the only place where William might have been born was at Becketts farm where Allen was living. Perhaps Elizabeth went to Arkesden for the birth. This is a possibility but seems unlikely in view of the fact that on both the census returns of 1861 and 1871 one or other of his parents recorded he was born in Camden Town, London, where he later went to school.

Florence Annie Dearsley was born at Stratton Park near Micheldever, Hampshire, on 10 December 1864, into a family of eight children, she being the last but one. The last child was a boy who died aged 3 months, the rest were girls. Florence's parents, David George Dearsley and Mary Collinson were both 'in service' when they married on 9 January 1851 in Syston, Lincolnshire. David continued in service throughout his working life, rising to be House Steward to the Duke of Grafton at Wakefield Lodge, Passenham, Northamptonshire. From this undoubtedly well paid employment he was able to maintain his large family in London at 65 Denbigh Street, Pimlico.

Florence Hurrell (née Dearsley).

Chapter 11

Above: The Horseshoe Hotel in Gwelo, Rhodesia (now Zimbabwe).

After a short stay in England, William returned to South Africa with Florence, drawn to the goldfields of Johannesburg where their first child, Grace, was born. It was not long before William was attracted to the newly occupied territory of Zambesia between the Limpopo and Zambezi rivers. The pioneer column had occupied the site of what was to become Salisbury (now Harare) in 1890. The territory was administered by the British South Africa Company with the entrepreneur Cecil Rhodes its visionary. The name was changed by proclamation to Rhodesia in 1895. When Rhodes gave approval for women to enter the territory, William with Florence and Grace trekked north by ox wagon, arriving in the vicinity of the settlement of Fort Victoria in October 1892. They were granted a settler's farm, which they named Arkesden, but a combination of blackwater fever, the Matabele War of 1893 and an outbreak of rinderpest caused them to up stakes and move to the new town of Gwelo (now Gweru) in the Midlands in 1895. Here their background in pubs and the

A later scene at the Horseshoe Hotel.

service industry no doubt influenced them to construct and open the Horseshoe Hotel, seen in these pictures, becoming coach agents for Zeederberg Coaches. Their first son, Dave, born on 17 April 1895, was the first white boy born in Gwelo and as a result was the recipient of a gift of 3,000 acres of land by Rhodes. William selected land in the Hunters Road area for his son and named it Foxton; later in 1915 he bought adjoining land and named it Harston.

In 1896, the Matabele and Mashona peoples rose in rebellion and the people of Gwelo went into 'laager', drawing a defensive line round part of the town into which all the townspeople moved. William had been active in the Matabele War of 1893 and in 1896 he took command of the Gwelo laager until a relief force arrived. It was at this time that William's activities came to the attention of Swann Hurrell, the 'Iron Duke' who expressed the desire to meet William.

Henry paid a short visit to Rhodesia at this time. A picture (upper right) taken of him shows that he was recruited as a combatant. But for his short visit to Rhodesia, Henry joined his mother in the running of the George and Dragon. In the last decade of the 19th century Henry was the Assistant Victualler at the pub. It was during this decade that Elizabeth had her picture taken at the

Henry A.C. Hurrell.

Elizabeth Hurrell (née Head).

Chapter 11

Henry A.C. Hurrell and Edith Stone – Wedding photograph.

Wandsworth Cemetery headstone inscription: Elizabeth Hurrell (née Head) and Henry A.C. Hurrell.

nearby studio of Alec Binnie in Putney. The picture is dated to about 1897 or 1898. On 5 July 1899, Henry Allen Conolly Hurrell married Edith Charlotte Stone in Holy Trinity Church, Hastings, Sussex. The two were photographed (see opposite page) at about the time of their wedding in Hastings.

Elizabeth died on 7 November 1900 and was buried in Wandsworth Cemetery, London. In Wandsworth, the *Borough News* paid a tribute to her on 17 November 1900.

> **Funeral of an Old Resident** – The funeral took place on Tuesday of Mrs Elizabeth Hurrell, widow of the late Mr Hurrell of the George and Dragon public house, West Hill. The deceased lady, who had resided in Wandsworth for the last 25 yrs, was, like her husband, greatly respected, and the last rites at the graveside in Wandsworth Cemetery were performed by the Rev Cunningham Craig in the presence of a large assemblage of mourners. The coffin which was literally covered in wreaths bore the inscription "In loving memory of Elizabeth Hurrell, died 7th November 1900, aged 64 yrs".

Edith Charlotte Stone was born on 12 February 1874 at 3 Gilbert Street, Grosvenor Square, London, into a family of nine children, she being the last child. Her father, Erasmus Stone, was a Master Tailor, an occupation which

Chapter 11

Henry A.C. Hurrell, seated right. One of the other two men is probably George Ostler.

was followed by three of her brothers. Erasmus was born about 1825 at Snitterton Hall, Matlock, Derbyshire, while her mother, Elizabeth, was born about 1827 in London. After Henry's mother Elizabeth's death, Henry and Edith continued to manage the George and Dragon with the help of George Ostler, barman. Their first and only child, Molly Elizabeth, was born on 28 January 1902 in Wandsworth. In 1903, shortly before the George and Dragon closed, Henry and two other men, most likely employees, had their photo taken: one of them may well have been George Ostler.

When the Boer War broke out in 1899, William joined Kitchener's Fighting Scouts under Colonel Colenbrander and Florence and the children went first to the Cape and then to

The Dearsley family group: Florence standing on the right.

England for the duration. A son, Rhodes, born 1897 had died a few months earlier. A third son, Stewart, was born in England. A Dearsley family photograph taken whilst they were in England shows Florence with her parents and three sisters, Georgina, Alice and Eleanor, together with her brothers-in-law as well as Grace, Dave and a cousin, Gladys Horn, seated on the ground in front. Florence is on the right of the group.

The Hurrells returned to Gwelo on 1 June 1902 and the next year Marjorie was born. The twins Geoffrey and Phyllis followed in 1905. William was Mayor of Gwelo several times, the last in 1925 at the time of the visit of the Prince of Wales. In 1927, the Horseshoe Hotel was sold and the family retired to Harston Farm. William, the Major, died on 16 April 1937 and was buried in Gwelo Cemetery. Florence lived the remainder of her life in Gwelo where she died on 28 March 1956.

The George and Dragon closed for business on 31 December 1903 and, in February 1904 Henry became tenant at Ye Olde Bull at 78 High Street, Wandsworth. But Henry did not live long; he died on 13 January 1906 aged 36 and is buried in Wandsworth Cemetery.

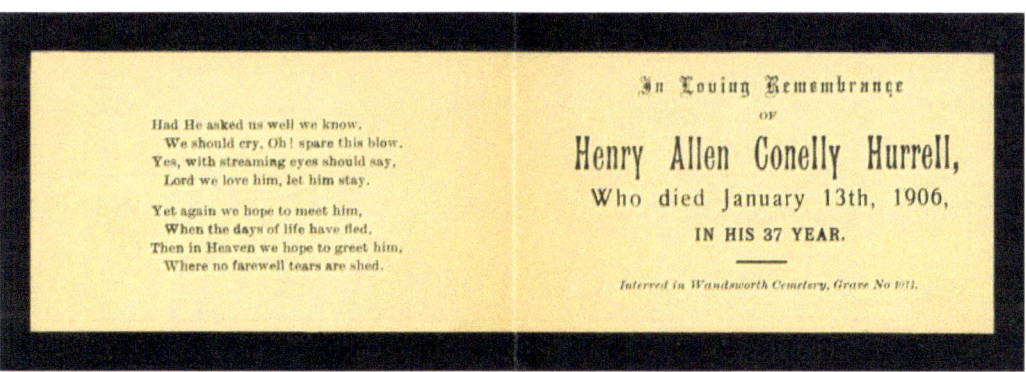

Edith married again, to James Field, and produced four more children. James and Edith continued to run Ye Olde Bull until 1910. From 1911 to 1925 they were in charge of The Earl Spencer in Merton Road, Wandsworth. Edith died on 14 December 1936 of pneumonia and carcinoma of the uterus. The passing of Edith ended the Hurrell's association with the Wandsworth pub scene, going back around 50 years.

Chapter 11

Edith Hurrell (née Stone) and Molly in 1903.

Descendants of this branch of the Hurrells multiplied in Rhodesia. Three more generations equally as enterprising as their forebears thrived and prospered. When Rhodesia became independent as Zimbabwe in 1982 it seemed as if life would go on as before, but tragically the Government of Robert Mugabe turned against the white settlers and opposition African parties with the result that unrest and violence turned into economic decline. The situation deteriorated to the point where the majority of the Hurrells have left Zimbabwe to find a better life elsewhere. They are now dispersed around the globe, in the United Kingdom, South Africa, Australia and America.

Of course the Hurrells of Newton and Harston never left England. They continued to prosper and still owned Manor farms and large estates well into the 20th century. Geoffrey Taylor Hurrell, Lord Lieutenant of Cambridgeshire from 1965 to 1975, still owned 300 acres at Harston in 1980. Meanwhile, Henry Allen Conolly's descendants, although not named Hurrell, also remained in England and prospered. The photograph above is of Edith and Molly, cousin of the Rhodesian family and only child of Henry and Edith. Molly was barely four when her father died. With Edith's marriage to James

Field, she grew up with her half brothers and sisters (see photograph below). The connection with the overseas Hurrells was broken: Molly became a 'lost' cousin to the descendants of Major William Hurrell. The story of all their lives must be left for others to write.

The Field family in 1916. L to R: James Field senior, Molly (Hurrell), James, Violet, Anne and Thomas on Edith Field's lap.

* * * * *

Appendix: Contents

Appendix 1	Sible Hedingham Hurrells: An Unfinished Story	109
Appendix 2	Lucy Gordon – Family Background	117
Appendix 3	Some other Descendants of Allen Hurrell and Lucy Gordon	125
Appendix 4	Elizabeth Hurrell Inventory, 1671	136
Appendix 5	Will of Allen Hurrell, (1698)	138
Appendix 6	Inventory of Allen Hurrell, (1700)	140
Appendix 7	Wills Referred to in this History	142
Appendix 8	Census Records Referred to in this History	144
Appendix 9	Documents in Relation to the Case in Chancery of Toplis v Hurrell	147
Bibliography		151

Appendix 1

Sible Hedingham Hurrells: An Unfinished Story

In the main chapters in this book all the relationships described are the results of rigorous researches. Where there is an element of doubt, it has been clearly indicated. It has, however, proved impossible to link George Hurrell (Chapter 2) to any other Hurrell families in or around the village of Sible Hedingham in Essex. The surviving parish records of births and burials were started in 1560 and marriages in 1599. Careful examination of these, the various Hurrell wills and other records held by the Essex Record Office in Chelmsford does, however, yield some interesting but incomplete information about these Hurrell families in the 1500s and early 1600s.

The earliest Hurrell family of Sible Hedingham so far identified is that of Roger Hurrell, his wife, Margaret, and their three children, William, Maud and Margaret, who were alive when Roger prepared his will[1] in 1540. He left his land, free and copyhold to his wife, Margaret, and after her death, to William. His daughters, Maud and Margaret, received 20 shillings each.

The oldest record so far found at the Essex R.O. about Sible Hedingham Hurrells, is dated 7 February 1525. This document[2] relates to lands, tenements and rents belonging to Bernard's Farm in Sible Hedingham, which was administered by Green and Herward's (Bernard's) Charity. Amongst those involved with its administration were John Hurrell (senior), William Hurrell (senior) and John Hurrell of Bloyes. There is nothing to suggest that John Hurrell of Bloyes was the son of John (senior).

A second document[3], dated 8 June 1525, deals with the transfer of land in Great Maplestead, which lies a couple of miles to the east of Sible Hedingham: one of those responsible is John Hurrell of Hurrontes in Sible Hedingham. How, and if, this John is related to the above two is unknown. The property Hurrontes does feature in later wills, as we shall see.

In another document[4], dated 4 January 1545, relating to a repairs clause in Green and Herward's (Bernard's) Charity, John Hurrell of Warners and William Hurrell (senior), as well as others, are named.

A fourth document[5], dated 21 February 1555 and endorsed 'Aldersford Almshouse', concerns rents that are to be distributed to the poor of Sible Hedingham. Once again there is Hurrell involvement; William Hurrell (senior) and Thomas Hurrell (senior).

In a fifth document[6], dated 26 November 1557, which also relates to lands, tenements and rents belonging to Bernard's Farm, there is reference to William Hurrell (yeoman), Thomas Hurrell, William Hurrell of Warners and Thomas Hurrell, son of William Hurrell. Here, at last, we have a relationship, but to which William? Warners was probably a manor house/farm, somewhere in or near to Sible Hedingham. It remained a Hurrell home for the rest of the 16th through the 17th and into the 18th century, ending in 1706 when the incumbent George Hurrell, William of Warners great-grandson, ordered its sale. Barnard's Farm, (modern spelling), still exists, two miles south-west of Sible Hedingham.

Already two features begin to emerge; firstly William, Thomas and John are names common within certain (but unspecified) Hurrell families, endorsing a trend evident in the earlier chapters in this book. The second feature relates to named properties: Bloyes, Hurrontes and Warners, which suggests that the families living in them had some social status, with a community involvement, in which the heads of household might describe themselves as yeomen farmers or even gentlemen, with some justification.

Bloyes or Blois Hall still stands, about two miles due west of Sible Hedingham. Adrian Corder-Birch, in his book *A Pictorial History of Sible Hedingham*, lists the ancient manors owned by the Lords of Hedingham Castle. Amongst these is Blois Hall, but there is no mention of Hurrontes or Warners. However, names do evolve: there is a farm called Warrens. Could Warners be a contraction of Warreners – a place where rabbits were bred?

John Hurrell of Hurrontes drew up his will[7] in February 1549. In it he names his wife, Amy, and three sons that survived him in this order: Robert, Richard and John, his eldest son. He left his *free tenement and land in Stisted* (a few miles to the south of Sible Hedingham and Halstead) to his wife, Amy. John is not clear in his will about the future of Hurrontes – he appears to leave it to his *well-beloved frende Giles Grey*. However, in her will[8] of January 1566, Amy leaves Hurrontes to her son, Richard. Her eldest son, John, might have been expected to inherit the farm, but did not, for reasons unknown. John was, however, the Executor of his mother's estate.

Of all the Hurrell families of Sible Hedingham in the late 1500s and early 1600s, those living at Warners provide the most detailed records. By the time William Hurrell of Warners had his will[9] drawn up in 1593, the property had been in the family for some decades, covering at least two earlier generations. William made no bequest to his wife; he must have died a widower, or made separate provision for her. He named his children as William (of Lamarsh, who inherited Warners), Thomas, Christopher, Nicholas, Morrice, Agnes and John. They would have been the contemporaries of George Hurrell's children (Chapter 2).

Some of William's children left detailed and informative wills. It is worth considering these wills carefully as it will illustrate some of the problems investigating the many Hurrell families of Sible Hedingham. His eldest son, William, although he inherited the family home of Warners, set up a new home in Lamarsh about 12 miles north-east of Sible Hedingham. His will[10] is dated 1612; the Lamarsh parish register reports his burial in April that year. So far information about William's brother Thomas has yet to be found. There is a 1616 will[11] drawn up for a Thomas Hurrell of Sible Hedingham. His wife was Allse, three children are named, but the names are not typical for the William Hurrell of Warners family line. He is unlikely to be the right Thomas.

From the baptisms register we can identify the children born to Christopher Hurrell: Joane (bpt 1569), Alice (1573), Christopher (1577), William (1585) and Thomas (1588). In his will[12], of 1626, Christopher names only his sons Christopher and Thomas, as well as his grandchild Joane Beagg. He makes no

Appendix 1

bequest to his wife, probably dying a widower. Christopher does not refer to any of his brothers or sister in the will.

The next of William of Warners' sons, Nicholas, drew up his will[13] in 1637. It is detailed and informative, full of penalty clauses in the event of default, and runs to five pages. He was married to Jeane, and at the time of his will, they had no surviving children. In his will he makes bequests to his wife and various nephews. Nicholas was a yeoman farmer and lived at Warners, the substantial family farm. The will tells us that his brother William, who had inherited Warners, was already dead. Nicholas' will also states that his late brother, William had lived at Lamarshe (modern spelling, Lamarsh). Perhaps he, William, did not take up his inheritance. Nicholas made a bequest to his nephew William, the son of his brother William (of Lamarshe). He also left Warners to Nicholas, another of William of Lamarshe's sons. Joan, William of Lamarshe's daughter, was left 40 shillings a year to be paid by Nicholas, her brother. Nicholas (senior) also made a bequest to his nephew, Moses, the son of his late brother Morrice.

The Sible Hedingham parish registers enable us to identify the children born to William of Warners' son, Morrice. Those named in Morrice's will[14] of 1626 are: Augustine or Austin (baptised 1577), Morris (1580), Mary (1583), Ann (1586) and Henry (1587). Of these it is worthwhile to follow the son, Morris a little further. Could this be the Morris who married Allyn Hurrell's sister, Rachell on 4 June 1604? If so it would link by marriage the Hurrells of Warners and the family of George Hurrell, Allyn and Rachell's father. Further examination of the baptisms shows this link to be very unlikely. The baptism register records that Moses, spelt Mousses, son of Morris, was baptised on 23 May 1602, two years before the Rachell Hurrell's marriage. It is therefore improbable that it was Moses' father who became Rachell's husband – unless his father became a widower shortly after Moses was born; but there is no evidence to support this.

Above: the baptism of Moses Hurrell, as in the Sible Hedingham parish register:
'Mousses hurrill sonne of morris h(urrill) was b(aptised) the xxiii day of may' (1602)
Note the two forms of the letter 's' as in Mousses, sonne and at the end of Morris. The letter 'r', (Hu<u>r</u>rell/Morris), is more like a modern 'v'. These letter-forms are typical of the time.

Identifying John, the son of William of Warners, presents a greater, and so far, unresolved challenge. There are wills drawn up by two John Hurrells in the 1590s, one in 1596 and the other in 1598. The first[15] had sons William and Edward (executor), and daughters Agnes and Parnell. He also mentions his daughter-in-law, Elizabeth, but does not state which of the sons she married. The second[16] John married Katheryn, and lived in a farm called Huntis or Huntes. Their surviving children were William, Jeane and John. The will[17] of the third John Hurrell, dated 1635, at first appears to be more promising. It is very detailed, naming Mary, his wife, sons John, William and Thomas, and daughters, Ann (Chandler) and Margaret (Levitt). The will shows that John had amassed considerable wealth; and this, together with the names – mostly good 'recycled' Hurrell names, indicates that he and his family could be descendants of William Hurrell of Warners. There is, however, a problem – and it is a big one – John leaves his brother William 40 shillings. We know from Nicholas's will of 1626 that brother William was already dead: so the third John is eliminated. William's death in 1612 is confirmed in the Lamarsh burial register.

The Hurrell families so far described are only part of the picture. In Chapter 2, detailed mention is made of the children of George Hurrell, but was limited to those cited in his will. The baptisms register shows that there may have been others: Grace (bpt 1560), Agnes (bpt 21 July 1561), William (May 1563), Thomas (July 1563), Susan (January 1564), Margh (October 1572), and Joane (May 1580). Examination of the register quickly shows a problem: Dorothie (see Chapter 2) was baptised on the 21 October 1562; William seven months later, Thomas after a further gap of two months, and Susan a (mere six months later. These are, of course, baptism, not birth dates, but it is possible that more than one George Hurrell family was involved. Furthermore only a few of the above names are found in the burial register. This increases the likelihood of additional, but unrecorded, George Hurrell families, although, so far, there is no other evidence to test this hypothesis.

The name George Hurrill also appears in a document[18] dated 22 May 1589, concerning the examination of witnesses about the liaison between one Margery Hawles, a married woman, and various men in Stambourne and nearby Sible Hedingham. Thomas Hurrill, of Stambourne, gives evidence, including information obtained from his wife and his brother, George Hurrill, *that John Stebbing told them that he had unlawfully to do with the said Margery Hawles twise in one night, and that she would have had him come to her a third time, which this examinant sayth they nowe denye again.* Although this George Hurrill had a brother, Thomas, there is insufficient evidence to conclude that he is the George Hurrell — father of Allyn and his siblings.

There is another Hurrell family with no identifiable connection to any of the Hurrell families heretofore mentioned: the family of Giles Hurrell. Between 1580 and 1594 there were five baptisms to Giles Hurrell and Urslie, his wife: Ursley (1580), John (1588), Rose (1590), Rachell (1593), and again Rachell (1594). Giles' wife, Urslie, was buried on 6 July 1601.

Between 1560 and 1620 the Sible Hedingham parish register lists 66 Hurrell baptisms and 27 Hurrell burials – a growing Hurrell population! Baptism number 65, in 1618, is that of Allin Hurrell, son of Rachell and Morrise. It was the first time the name Allin, including variants, born into any family, Hurrell or otherwise, was recorded in the Sible Hedingham baptism register, since its inception in 1560. Clearly Allin, Allyn or Allen were then rarely used names. Allyn, son of George, was probably the first instance of an Allyn Hurrell in the lineage described in this book. Furthermore the name appears not to have been used by any of the other Hurrell families. Allyn Hurrell, in his will[19] of 1623, mentions his uncle *Francis Hunicke* (Hunwick), and his children Allin and Ellyn Hunicke. That this Francis Hunwick was one of the brothers of George's wife, Agnes, is almost certain, and it would be reasonable to assume that the name Allyn entered the Hurrell line from the Hunwicks.

The better known but smaller village of Castle Hedingham, with its imposing Norman keep, sits a short walk from Sible Hedingham on the opposite bank of the River Colne. Marriage records for St Nicholas, the parish church in Castle Hedingham, date from 1559. However, there is no marriage involving a Hurrell prior to 1632, when on 9th August, one Nicholas Hurrill married Jane Curry. It seems that the early Hurrells living in and around Sible Hedingham were, for many decades, loyal to its church, St Peter's.

So much remains to be discovered. Although some Hurrell families have been identified in this appendix, we simply do not know how many others lived within a few miles of Sible Hedingham. Information in wills does not always shed much light: Rachell Hurrell of Sible Hedingham – probably not one of the Rachells encountered earlier – wrote her will[20] in 1639, in which she names Thomas Hurrell, his wife, Susan, and their daughter, Susan. Presumably Thomas is related to Rachell, but this remains unspecified. All three are alive when the will was dawn up. There is, however, a marriage of Thomas Hurrell to Susan Masson in 1612, and the burial of Susan, wife of Thomas Hurrell an 1624. As we have said, Thomas was a common Hurrell name, and we do not know how many Thomas Hurrell families were living at the time.

In the Preface to this book we are reminded of Swann Hurrell's assertion that a branch of the Hurrells – the 'North Essex' branch – moved, around 1590, from Sible Hedingham to the area around Bulmer and Brundon Hall, near Sudbury; and another, the 'Eldest' branch settled, around 1700, in Boreham and Malden Heybridge in Essex. Research carried out up to the time that this book went to press has not linked either of these branches to any of the named Hurrell families of Sible Hedingham. The 'Youngest' branch which settled in Foxton, Harston and Newton, Cambs, c1590, has now been linked back to George Hurrell.

The rapid increase in the number of Hurrells in and around Sible Hedingham during the reign of Elizabeth I would have resulted in a drift away from the village. There is evidence of Hurrells living in surrounding villages in the 1600s. The Elizabethan era was a time of good health and expansion – in which the Hurrells, no doubt, played their part. Swann Hurrell's 'branched' exodus probably applied to particular, perhaps wealthy, Hurrell families, and may have been part of a wider pattern of migration as families sought new farms to work and places to live, by necessity, further afield.

Much more research needs to be done, with some lucky discoveries of hitherto unseen documents, before the history of the Hurrells of Sible Hedingham is more fully understood. If one explores the documents held by the Essex Record Office – many are available online – it is clear that the early Hurrells were a significant part of life in and around Sible Hedingham. During the 17th and 18th centuries as their numbers grew they spread further into the surrounding towns and villages, and some, further afield – to Cambridgeshire, and in the 19th century to London and southern Africa. Later, the number remaining declined: the 1841 census forms list just three Hurrell families in Sible Hedingham — agricultural labourers and weavers, 13 souls in all. By 1861 there was just one Hurrell left, Jonathan, aged 62. Ten years later there were none. An odd feature of Adrian Corder-Birch's *A Pictorial History of Sible Hedingham* is that there is not a single reference to the Hurrell name!

A footnote to this appendix: a study of the modern Ordnance Survey 2.5 inch to the mile Explorer map (sheet 195) reveals the locations of Blois Hall and

Appendix 1

Barnards. The nearest farm called Warrens is some 10 miles to the north-west of Sible Hedingham. The village of Toppesfield became the home of some Hurrells in the 17th century. About one mile south-west of that village is Hurall's Farm. The small rural community of Little Maplestead lies three miles east of Sible Hedingham. Within the village there is a farm named Hurrell's Farm. Whether either of these two farms have links to the Hurrell line described in this book has yet to be discovered.

References in this appendix:
- (1) Essex R.O. D/ABW 18/78   [Roger Hurrell 1540]
- (2) Essex R.O. T/A 225/1
- (3) Essex R.O. D/DHt/T523
- (4) Essex R.O. T/A 225/3
- (5) Essex R.O. T/A 225/38
- (6) Essex R.O. T/A 225/4
- (7) Essex R.O. D/ABW 18/91   [John Hurrell of Hurrontes 1568/9]
- (8) National Archives PROB 11/50   [Amy Hurrell]
- (9) Essex R.O. D/ABW 19/235   [William Hurrell of Warners 1593]
- (10) Essex R.O. D/ABW 20/182   [William Hurrell of Lamarsh 1612]
- (11) Essex R.O. D/ABW 20/272   [Thomas Hurrell 1616]
- (12) Essex R.O. D/ABW 49/284   [Christopher Hurrell]
- (13) Essex R.O. D/ABW 55/28   [Nicholas Hurrell]
- (14) Essex R.O. D/ABW 50/213   [Morris Hurrell]
- (15) Essex R.O. D/ABW 19/301   [John Hurrell 1596]
- (16) Essex R.O. D/ABW 19/317   [John Hurrell 1598]
- (17) Essex R.O. D/ABW 53/30   [John Hurrell 1635]
- (18) Essex R.O. Q/SR 109/62a
- (19) National Archives PROB 11/142 [Allin Hurrell 1623]
- (20) Essex R.O. D/ABW 56/99   [Rachell Hurrell 1639]

Appendix 2

Lucy Gordon – Family Background

The family background of Lucy Gordon, who married Allen Hurrell of Arkesden in 1813 and lived at Hobs Aerie, remained a mystery until early in 2009 when Lesley Bone traced her forebears to the Cranmer Gordons and ultimately to the Cranmers of Quendon Hall, Quendon, in Essex (about four miles from Arkesden). The story that unfolded is so colourful that it is considered worth recording. Although no baptismal or birth records have been found for Lucy Gordon, three clues placed her in the Cranmer family. Firstly, her husband, Allen Hurrell, was one of two 'Sureties' to the Bond of Lucy's brother, Henry Cranmer Gordon, in his application to join the British East India Company in 1818 as a Free Mariner. Secondly, another brother, James Stewart Gordon Cranmer, a clergyman, baptised the children of Lucy's son William, the father of the Major in 1867. Thirdly, Lucy's mother, Lucy Cranmer Gordon, died in the home of her daughter's son-in-law Henry Toplis at 8 Frederick Street, Hampstead (Road), London, on 6 January 1848.

Probably, Lucy Gordon was the first of nine children of Joseph Cranmer Gordon, a surgeon, by all accounts the illegitimate son of Henry Cranmer of

Quendon Hall. Up to Henry Cranmer's generation the family name was Cranmer. The name Gordon was sometimes combined with Cranmer in the next generation. Thus it seems possible that Henry Cranmer's liaison was with a Gordon. To ensure maximum confusion the name was variously Cranmer Gordon, Gordon Cranmer and sometimes just Gordon. And, as we shall see, some of Lucy's siblings later claimed that Gordon was just an assumed name!

The story unfolded in parish records, records held at the Essex Record Office in Chelmsford, reports in *The Times* newspaper of the Court of Chancery sittings, and in letters to the Editor of the *Sunday Herald*. It is a story of a family divided.

Henry Cranmer was born about 1730 in London and died on 24 December 1810 in Quendon. His son Joseph Cranmer Gordon, probably illegitimate, was baptised on 6 May 1770. Joseph married Lucy (maiden name unknown) and they had nine children between 1790 and 1807. The first was Lucy, wife of Allen Hurrell, born about 1790, and died in 1849; next Henry Cranmer Gordon, 1794–1842, died in Bengal, India; then William Cranmer Gordon, born 1796, died after 1826; James Stewart Gordon Cranmer, born 1800, died between 1871 and 1881; Richard Cranmer Gordon, 1802–1845; John Cranmer Gordon, born 1804; and Joseph Cranmer Gordon, born 1807, died between 1861 and 1871. Joseph Cranmer Gordon was preceded by a child of the same name who died in infancy before 1807 and there was another daughter named Maria Gordon, born around 1800, who later married a George Canning and was involved with her brothers in disputation over the inheritance.

On 29 July 1806 a Commission of Lunacy was established, followed by an enquiry which found Henry Cranmer to be of unsound mind and unable to govern his own estates – in the legal terminology of that time he was declared a lunatic. In keeping with the bizarre nature of this history, just before the Commission of Lunacy, Henry Cranmer had been abducted from his estate and taken to London by a James Winton and Mrs Greygoose (reported in the press as Mrs Winston). They were activated in the hope of possessing his property. Henry was found at an address in Camden Town and extracted by the Bow-Street Officers with difficulty in the face of Mrs 'Winston'. The case came before the Court of Chancery. At the Commission of Lunacy James Winton appeared with the lunatic armed with sword and pistol. He was arrested and eventually gaoled.

Children and Grandchildren of Henry Cranmer and Margaret

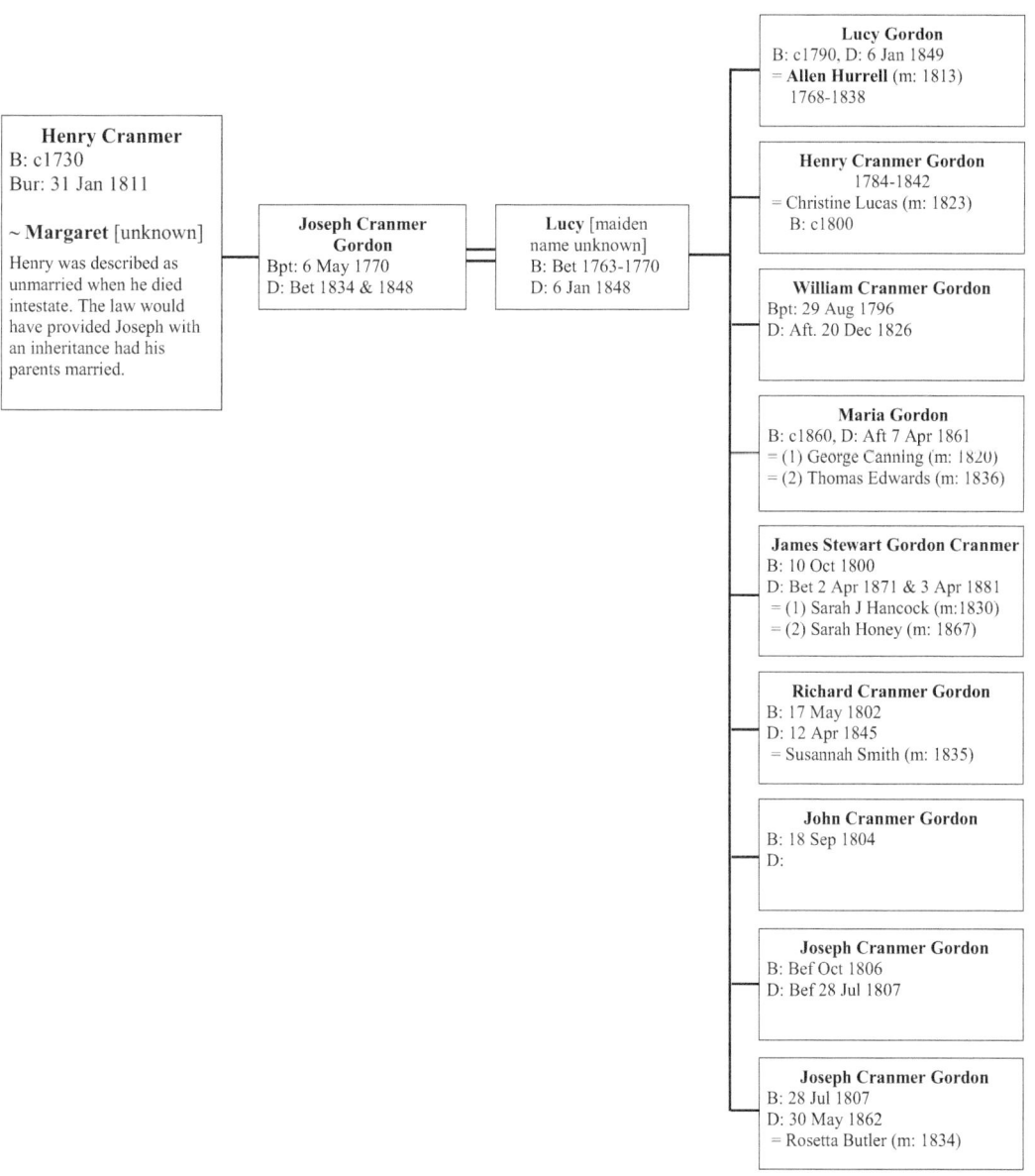

In December of that year, James Powell Mouncey Esq, Solicitor, the receiver appointed to the lunatic's estate, named the Reverend Robert Cranmer, Henry's first cousin, heir at law and next of kin. Among other cousins named as next of kin was Robert's sister, Martha Cranmer. The illegitimate son, Joseph Cranmer Gordon was not named. However, it was agreed that Robert Cranmer would look after the estates of the lunatic and Joseph Cranmer Gordon would look after the person of the lunatic. Joseph, commissioned a lieutenant in the West Essex Militia in 1803, had been reared and supported by his father, Henry, by frequent remittances of money, but when these supplies were withheld Joseph discovered the Wintons had intruded into his family. It is evident that the Wintons had been living at Quendon Hall for some time prior to 1806. When the Commission of Lunacy was established the Wintons were ejected and Joseph returned to Quendon Hall to look after his father. Joseph's appointment to look after Henry at Quendon gave great umbrage to Mr Winton who wrote an insolent letter to Joseph seeking a meeting with him, clearly intending to provoke him to fight a duel. A charge of criminal information was brought against Winton in the Court of King's Bench in November 1806. Mrs Winton continued to make claims against Henry Cranmer's estate involving paying off a mortgage debt, until 1814.

The heir at law Robert Cranmer died in 1809 and the estate passed to his sister Martha Cranmer. At the death of Henry Cranmer in 1810, Mr Mouncey, the Solicitor, gave Joseph Cranmer Gordon notice to quit Quendon Hall as Martha Cranmer was going to occupy the farm. Joseph believed the farm was in a better state in 1810 than when he arrived in 1806.

Joseph Cranmer Gordon himself led an extravagant life and had a chequered career as evidently he ran away with his wife Lucy's servant-maid, claiming that others like the Prince of Wales, the Duke of York and the Duke of Queensbury have their mistresses so why shouldn't he? Martha Cranmer died two years after inheriting Quendon Hall and willed the property to Ann Webb, referred to as 'an attendant', who was also a relation of her's. Ann Webb shortly after married Mr Mouncey, the Solicitor, who was now the Steward at Quendon, and they then took the name of Cranmer! By 1834 they had enjoyed the property for over 20 years.

In 1834, three descendants of Joseph Cranmer Gordon wrote to the Sunday Herald aiming to establish their claim to the estates of Henry Cranmer. Three brothers, James Stewart, Joseph and Richard along with old Joseph senior (then living in the parish of Hackney), signing themselves as Cranmer only, sent a letter to the Editor making the claim that Joseph senior was the son and proper claimant to the estates of the late Henry Cranmer of Quendon Hall. In support of this they claimed that Gordon was just an assumed name of their father and that he was in fact the lawful son of Henry and Margaret Cranmer of Quendon Hall. The newspaper later regretted printing the letter in view of the fact that the writers had suppressed the knowledge that Joseph Cranmer Gordon (the Joseph Cranmer Senior of the letter) was only the illegitimate son of Henry Cranmer and not his lawful heir. At about the same time James, under his second name Stewart, exhibited a paper in the Public Library at Bishops Stortford charging Mr Mouncey (now Cranmer) with having kept back from his father money due to him from the family estates; also charging him with having, by unjust and improper means, obtained possession of the family estates. A case brought in the King's Bench against Stewart was refused. And there the matter seemed to end without any satisfaction to the Cranmer Gordons. One cannot help thinking that Lucy Gordon, married to Allen Hurrell, kept out of the argument as much as possible.

Shortly before these events, in May 1834, Maria Canning (née Gordon), sister of Lucy Gordon, was involved in a much publicized and extraordinary case of outrage and extortion. Maria's husband, George Canning, who incidentally was the cousin of John Cater Canning of the Hurrell Chancery case, had died six years previously. He left £2,000 in the hands of a Mr Gee, Attorney, to be invested for Maria and her three daughter's benefit so long as she remained a widow. Up to this point £1,200 had been invested, leaving £800 in the hands of Mr Gee. Maria had recently undergone a marriage ceremony with a blind friend, Thomas Edwards, under the assumed name of Maria West (no doubt to avoid losing the inheritance). What followed was apparently a plot by Thomas Edwards alone, without the connivance of Maria, to get his hands on the remaining money and investments to enable all of them to get to America. With this in mind, Edwards, with the help of two associates, enticed Mr Gee to his house where they caught hold of him and confined him chained and bound in a small sound-proofed den and threatened not to release him until

Mrs Maria Canning.

he produced a cheque for £800 and an order for the delivery of the deeds of the property in which the £1,200 had been invested. Mr Gee, in fear for his life, complied with the request, but when he had been left alone, managed to break out of the den. As a result Edwards and his two associates were arrested and brought before the magistrates. After many witnesses and much evidence the prisoners were committed to trial at Newgate on a charge of stealing money by menaces and force. In the end it was accepted that Edwards did not intend to do Mr Gee an injury and his motivation was to help Maria Canning and not himself. It seems that Edwards got off with a misdemeanor and two years later he married Maria Canning under her real name. What became of the investments is not known.

* * *

It is known from the *Surrey Herald* in 1834 that Joseph Cranmer Gordon, had left his wife Lucy, and ran off with her servant-maid. It is believed that she was called Mary Ann. Further research has established that a Joseph Cranmer Gordon and Mary Ann had five children. A family chart is shown opposite.

While there is no proof that Mary Ann was the servant in question, the fact that she was born in Quendon, Essex, and that her son was given the middle name Cranmer, shows that she is most probably the right person. Her maiden surname, however, remains undiscovered.

Only one death certificate for a Joseph Cranmer Gordon has been found, and, whilst it raises more questions than it solves, it is believed that it is for the same Joseph Cranmer Gordon who was married to Lucy, and also had a family with Mary Ann.

Joseph Cranmer Gordon died in St Albans, Hertfordshire, in December 1851. However, his marital status is not clear from his death certificate. On his wife Lucy's death certificate in 1848 she is shown as a widow. This leads to the assumption that her husband had predeceased her. The witness to her death was not a family member, and may not have known whether Joseph Cranmer Gordon was alive or not. In the 1851 census Mary Ann is living in with her daughter and her family in Hackney. She states that she is married, but no marriage has been found in the period from Lucy's death and the 1851 census. In both the 1841 and 1851 census, Joseph Cranmer Gordon is living in St Albans.

* * * * *

Lucy Gordon – Family Background

Children of Joseph Cranmer Gordon and Mary Ann ——

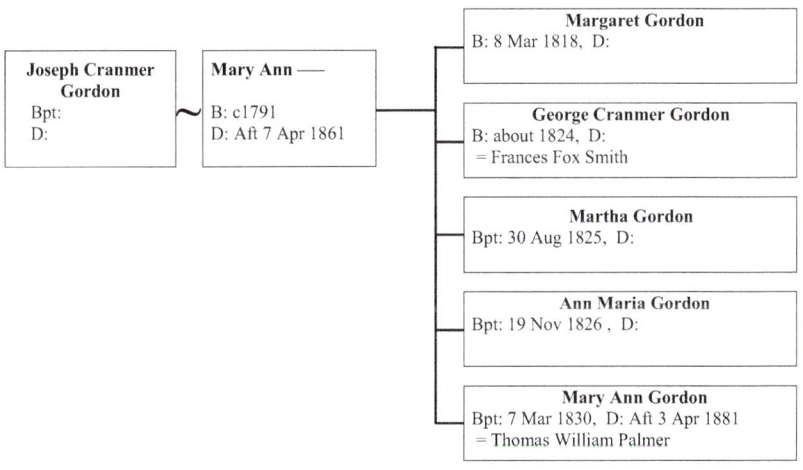

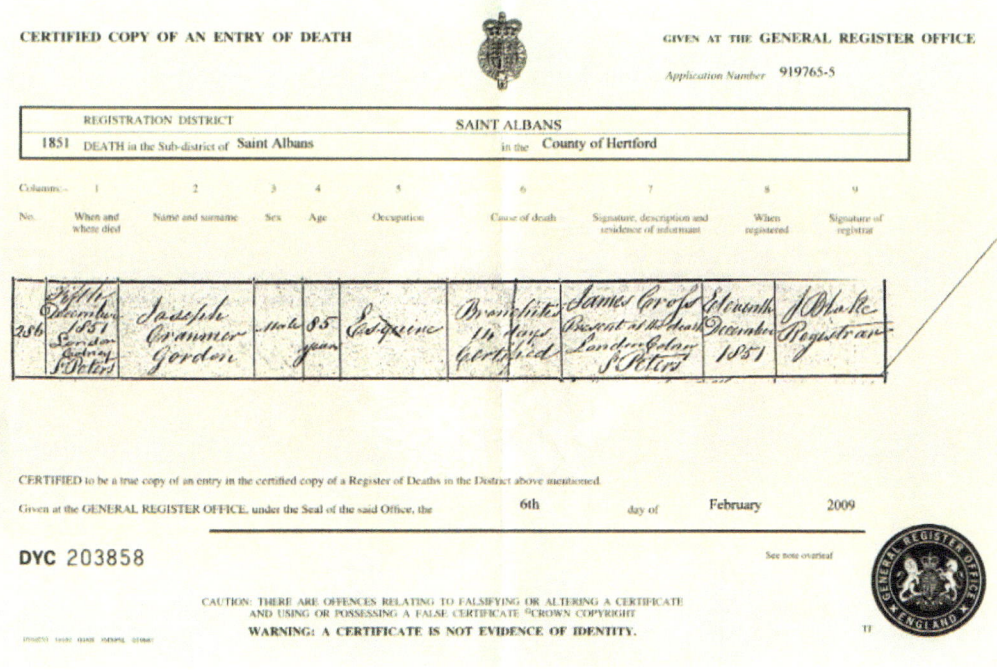

Death certificate of Joseph Cranmer Gordon, dated 5 December 1851.

Appendix 2

Quendon Church.

Quendon Church plaques: (left) Martha Cranmer, (right) James Powell Cranmer, formerly Mouncey, and his wife, Anne Cranmer.

Appendix 3

Some other Descendants of Allen Hurrell and Lucy Gordon

During the research into the Cambridgeshire Hurrells it has become obvious that there are very few descendants of Allen Hurrell and Lucy Gordon, apart from the authors' own line described earlier in this book.

In the following pages a few descendants have been highlighted, some because what actually happened to them is not known, and others because they have left a very clear and visible mark in the modern world.

1. **Children of Allen Hurrell and Mary Bailey** (see charts, p52 and p126):

Allen Hurrell, born 1853, married Elizabeth Matilda Smith on 30 June 1878 in Shadwell Middlesex.

Records have been found of five children born to this couple. Two of the sons, born in 1882 and 1886, both named Allen, died young. Another, Arthur James Hurrell, died in 1918. This leaves two children Elizabeth Annie Hurrell, and William Hurrell, who were both alive at the time of the 1911 census, when they were living together in Leytonstone, Essex.

William Bailey Hurrell born 1861, disappeared from view after the 1871 census, when he was at home, aged 10 in Arkesden.

Appendix 3

Children of Allen Hurrell and Mary Bailey

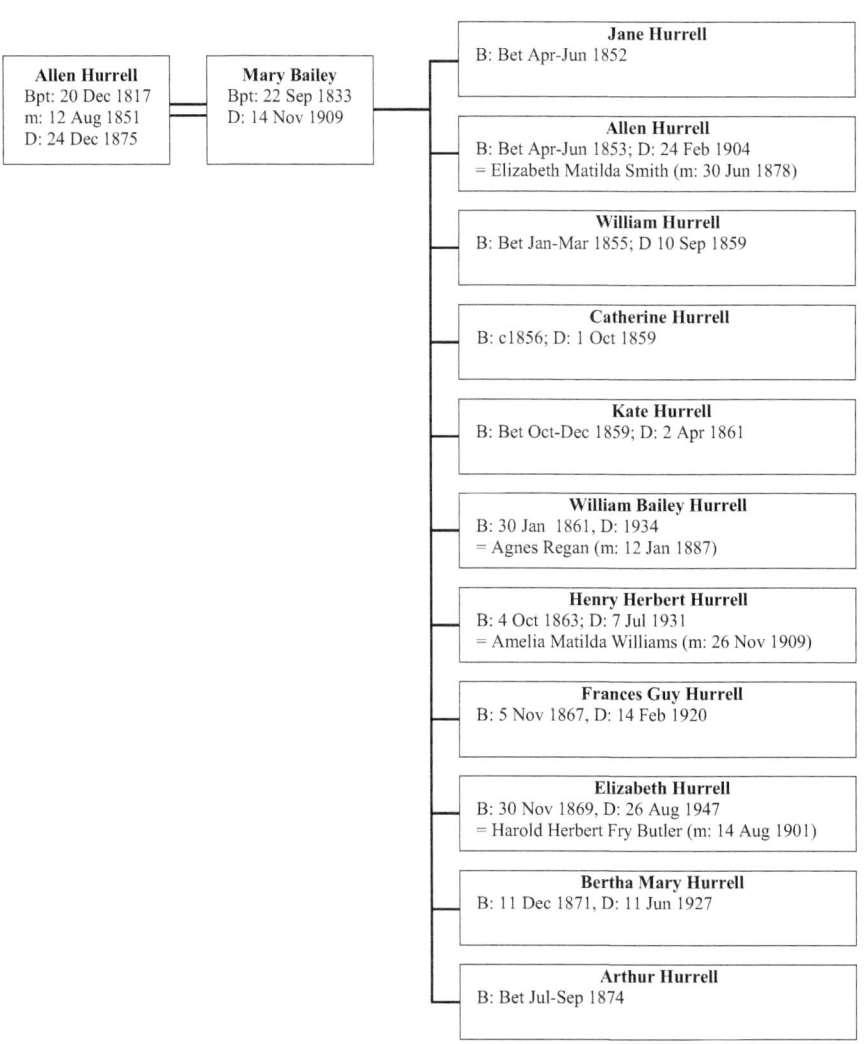

Allen Hurrell
Bpt: 20 Dec 1817
m: 12 Aug 1851
D: 24 Dec 1875

Mary Bailey
Bpt: 22 Sep 1833
D: 14 Nov 1909

Jane Hurrell
B: Bet Apr-Jun 1852

Allen Hurrell
B: Bet Apr-Jun 1853; D: 24 Feb 1904
= Elizabeth Matilda Smith (m: 30 Jun 1878)

William Hurrell
B: Bet Jan-Mar 1855; D 10 Sep 1859

Catherine Hurrell
B: c1856; D: 1 Oct 1859

Kate Hurrell
B: Bet Oct-Dec 1859; D: 2 Apr 1861

William Bailey Hurrell
B: 30 Jan 1861, D: 1934
= Agnes Regan (m: 12 Jan 1887)

Henry Herbert Hurrell
B: 4 Oct 1863; D: 7 Jul 1931
= Amelia Matilda Williams (m: 26 Nov 1909)

Frances Guy Hurrell
B: 5 Nov 1867, D: 14 Feb 1920

Elizabeth Hurrell
B: 30 Nov 1869, D: 26 Aug 1947
= Harold Herbert Fry Butler (m: 14 Aug 1901)

Bertha Mary Hurrell
B: 11 Dec 1871, D: 11 Jun 1927

Arthur Hurrell
B: Bet Jul-Sep 1874

The following message was placed on a genealogical website in 2006 by Michael & Lynne Ball:

William B HURRELL is shown as having been born in Essex in 1861 from his Shipping Discharge papers... joined up as BOY in 1877 aged 16 and discharged in Sydney in 1882 where he settled and form part of our family tree... Have you got a sibling on your family tree that fits this info that leads nowhere!!!

It was immediately apparent that this could be our William Bailey Hurrell, however what did the 'B' stand for in the Australian William B Hurrell?

Above: Certificate of the marriage of William Bailey Hurrell and Agnes Regan, dated 12 January 1887, New South Wales. (This copy issued in 2006.)

Left: A Certificate of Discharge in the name of W. B. Hurrell, Boy, of Essex, dated 31 December 1877, from the trading ship 'Rainbow', registered in London. The next day he signed on again, as W. Hurrell, Seaman, on the Rainbow, trading between London and Hamburg. His second discharge paper is dated 17 August 1878.

Over the next year Michael and Lynne ordered certificates to try and discover what the initial B stood for. At long last a marriage certificate, dated 1887, showed that William Bailey Hurrell married Agnes Regan. It is almost certain that this William Bailey Hurrell was the young 10-year-old who disappeared after the 1871 census!

William Bailey Hurrell and Agnes Regan only had one child, Elizabeth Hurrell, born 1889, who married Hilton John McGill in 1912, and all her descendants, including grand-daughter Sandra, either lived or live in Australia.

Henry Herbert Hurrell, born in 1863, married Amelia Matilda Williams in 1909. By the time of the 1911 census Henry and Amelia had had one child, who did not survive. Henry Herbert Hurrell was a chemist and died in 1931. There are no known surviving issue of this couple.

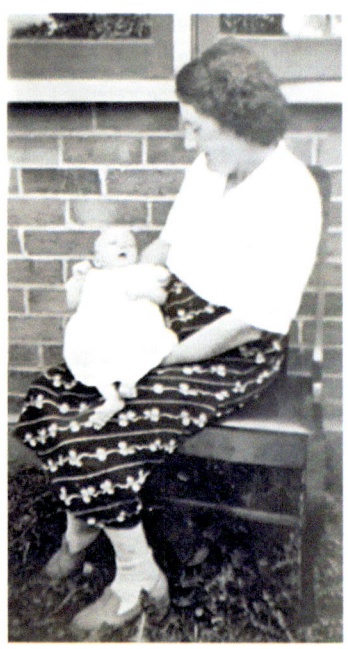

Elizabeth McGill (née Hurrell) and grand-daughter, Sandra.

Elizabeth Hurrell, born 1869, married Harold Herbert Fry Butler in 1901. Harold Butler worked for Westminster City Council as a public health official. Elizabeth paid for the recasting of the tenor bell in Arkesden Church. A plaque marks the event:

The tenor bell in the Belfry was recast and re-hung by Elizabeth Butler in December 1931 in loving memory of her mother, Mary Hurrell, late of this parish.

Elizabeth, who had no children, died in 1947 in Guildford, Surrey.

The plaque marking the recasting of the tenor bell at Arkesden Church in memory of Mary Hurrell.

There are two children of Allen Hurrell and Mary Bailey, who have not been traced into their adult lives. The eldest child, **Jane Hurrell**, was born 1852 in Arkesden, Essex. In the 1871 census, Jane was working in London as a nurse, aged 18 years. Nothing further has been discovered about her. The youngest child, **Arthur Hurrell** was born 1874 in Poplar, Middlesex. In the 1891 census, Arthur was still living at home, also aged 18 years, a printer by trade. Again nothing is known about Arthur's adult life.

Arkesden churchyard: the headstone (top right) and inscription at the grave of Allen Hurrell, his wife Mary and three of their children, William, Catherine and Kate.

2. **Children of George Archibald Cranmer and Fanny Hurrell** (from chart, p52):

Ethel Annie Worthington Cranmer was born 28 June 1865 and died 21 Feb 1927 in Brighton, Sussex, aged 62. She was buried with her mother at Kensal Green Cemetery, London.

The £300 that Ethel used to set up the Hurrell Cranmer Epiphany Trust Fund in 1917, mentioned towards the end of Chapter 9, was only a small portion of a considerable fortune she had amassed. Perhaps the interest from the £300 invested was insufficient to meet the aims of the Fund to provide for the poor of Arkesden and to maintain the Hurrell family tomb there, as a result, the capital was spent. This bequest is however significant, representing a continuing interest in Arkesden by the Hurrells long after they left the village.

Ethel's next gift, this time to support her local church, St Mary's, in Brighton, was made through her will in 1927. In it she bequeathed a large sum of money to the church. Although her will has not been read, it is known that she left

The stone altar in St. Mary's Church, Brighton, in memory of Ethel Annie Worthington Cranmer.

an estate of £13,136 12s 9d. Her bequest to the church included funds for an oak screen to be erected at the back of the choir stalls, for the creation of a choir vestry, and for a carved stone altar in the sanctuary, all in her memory. All her wishes were carried out. The altar, made of Caen stone is magnificent and replaced an old wooden altar.

The grave of Fanny and Ethel Cranmer, with inscriptions, in Kensal Green Cemetery, London, photo taken in 1998.

Appendix 3

Children and grandchildren of Maria Hurrell and Augustin King George

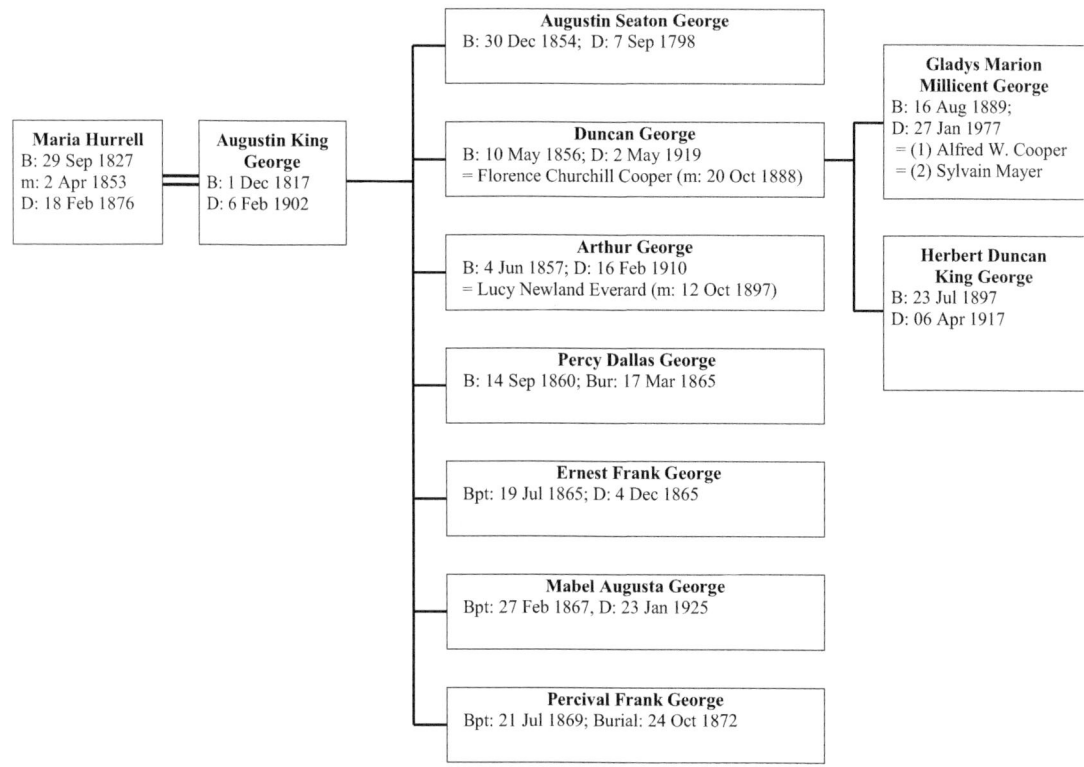

3. Children of Augustin King George and Maria Hurrell
(see charts, p52 and p132):

Duncan George was born in 1856 and in 1888 he married Florence Churchill Cooper in Bengal, India. They had two children, Gladys and Herbert, both born in India. Gladys Marion Millicent George married her cousin, Alfred William Cooper in Marseilles, France in June 1928. In 1946, she married a KC, Sylvain Mayer. Gladys died on 27 January 1977 in Ealing, London, with no known issue. Herbert Duncan King George was born on 23 July 1897 and died whilst a prisoner of war on 6 Apr 1917 in German hands. He was a Lieutenant in the Royal Dublin Fusiliers, having only been promoted one month before he went to France. He is commemorated at Douai Communal Cemetery, France. His Record of Service has yet to be discovered, but his Medal Card shows that he entered France on 29 March 1916.

Arthur George was born in 1857 and in 1897 married Lucy Newland Everard.

He was a Major in the 1st Battalion, North Staffordshire Regiment and died in 1910. He is buried at Bardon, Leicestershire with his wife, who died in 1914.

The overgrown family vaults of two George families — Augustin King George and his son, Duncan George. The base edging of the tombs carries the inscriptions:

Below left: 'The Family Vault of A K George Esq'.

Below right: 'The Family Vault of Duncan George [Esq]'.

Appendix 3

4. **Children and descendants of Elizabeth Ann Hurrell** (from chart, p 80):

Elizabeth Ann Hurrell, born 1859 to William Hurrell and Elizabeth Head, was married twice. In 1878 she married John Byles and, while no record of his death has been found, he was the youngest of nine children and worked as a Railway Clerk. They had one daughter, Florence Annie.

Florence Annie Byles, born 1879, married Clifford Haigh Halcrow in 1901. Florence and Clifford had eight children between 1901 and 1923. They have many descendants. Florence died in 1968 — having maintained contact with the Hurrell family in Rhodesia. Her aunt Mary (Pollie) Hurrell went out to Rhodesia after her husband Edwin Alfred Hadden died in 1893. Mary married Henry Kennedy Smyth in 1897. Florence was left £500 in Henry's will in 1952.

Elizabeth married again in 1888 to William Nicholls Dunn. They had one daughter, Ethel Annie. However this marriage was to be short lived as Elizabeth died in 1897 and William in 1899.

Florence Halcrow (née Byles) with members of her family.

John Charles Bayles and Ethel Annie (née Dunn).

Ethel Annie Dunn born 1887 married John Charles Bayles in 1916. Following the death of her parents, Ethel was brought up by her aunt, Alma Everett, and was still living with her in the 1911 census. Ethel had two children and there are living descendants.

It is almost certain that the half sisters, Florence and Ethel, never knew each other.

Elizabeth Ann Hurrell and William Nicholls Dunn are buried together in Wandsworth Cemetery, London. Their grave (left) is next to her mother Elizabeth (née Head) and brother Henry A. C. Hurrell's grave (right). The inscription on Elizabeth and William's grave has now become illegible.

Appendix 4

An Inventory of the Goods and Chattels of Elizabeth Hurrell of Harston, 1671

July ye 5 1671

	£	s.	d.	Line
An Invitory of ye Goods and Chattels of Elizabeth Hurrell of				1
Harston in the County of Cambridge widow as ffolloweth				2
Imprimis in ye Chamber over ye Hall her wereing apparel				3
and money in her Pocket - - - - - - -	12	0	0	4
In the same roome one halfe headed bed 2 flockbeds one feather				5
bowster and two feather pillows one coverlead[1] and one blanket -	1	10	0	6
In ye same roome 3 Chests one trunck and 2 tables - - -	1	0	0	7
In ye same roome 6 paire of flaxen sheets 5 paire of hempen sheets				8
2 long table cloths and a short one 3 dussen of fflaxen napkins one dussen				9
of pillowbeers[2] 8 fflaxen and 4 hempen with one perch of lining yarn -	9	10	0	10
two rideing suits one Pillian[3] and Cloth - - - - -	1	0	0	11
In ye roome over the parlor in bonds fouer score and ten pounds -	90	0	0	12
In money due upon accompts - - - - - - -	10	0	0	13
One gold ring and one sillver bowll - - - - - -	3	0	0	14
In ye same roome 3 Chests and a box one chaire one stoolles				15
one trundlebed 2 blanketts and a feather bowster - - -	1	5	0	16
In ye Palor one joyne[4] bed one trundlebed 2 feather beds[5] 2 feather				17
bowsters 2 pillows 2 blankets one rug one coverlead and one pair				18
of curtains - - - - - - - - -	8	0	0	19
In the same roome 2 livery Cubberds and a joine Chair				20
with 2 cubert cloths - - - - - - - -	1	6	8	21
In the same roome 2 joyne Chairs 2 rush Chairs one wicker				22
Chair and 2 stooles one lookenglace[6] one Carpet 10 Cussions				23
one forme[7] - - - - - - - - -		5	0	24
In the same roome one Cubberd 4 rush Chairs and a joine Chair				25
and one Cubberd cloath 2 bibles - - - - - -		18	0	26
In ye Kitchin one brasse pott one bellmettle[8] pott one paire of				27
andirons[9] 2 paire of tongs one Brasse scimer[10] 2 spitts				28
2 drippinpans one flitch[11] of bacon one mortar - - -	5	6	8	29
In ye same roome 4 bottles 2 scillets[12] one warming pan				30
one paire of brasse Cobbirons[13] one brasse basson on(e) brass				31
Chafindish[14] one basting ladle - - - - - -		18	0	32
In ye same roome one kneding trofe[15] 2 sives one kimnell[16]				33

Inventory of Goods and Chattels of Elizabeth Hurrell of Harston, 1671

	£	s	d	
2 boshells of wheat 13 winter dishes 2 candlesticks a dussen of spo(o)ns				34
one fflaggon and one Chamberpot 2 salts - - - - - -	2	0	0	35
In ye dairy one Cheespres[17] one powderin tub one powderin trof[18]				36
5 shelves with other lumber - - - - - - -	1	10	0	37
In ye drink buttery 4 barrills 4 tubs with other lumber - - -	1	10	0	38
In ye chamber over the daray 4 ffleces of wooll one potshelle[19]				39
3 wheells[20] and a roll with other lumber - - - - -		18	0	40
In ye yard 2 cows and one hog - - - - - -	6	6	0	41
two Rid hins and one cock - - - - - - -		8	8	42
one logge and ye dung in ye yard - - - - - -		10	0	43
One parcel of cheese - - - - - - -	1	0	0	45
The fruit in ye orchard and cloce - - - - - -	1	10	0	46
The hay in ye Close - - - - - - -	1	0	0	47
	166	10	0	48

(Signed)　　Henry Greenell

　　　　　　　John Bonner

Notes:

(1) Coverlead: bedcover, bedspread
(2) Pillowbeers: pillowcases
(3) Pillian/pillion: (hist) a woman's light saddle or a cushion attached to the back of a saddle for a second rider
(4) Joyne/joine: item made by a joiner, eg table, stool bedstead or chair with legs joined at the top
(5) Featherbed: feather filled mattress
(6) Lookenglace: looking glass or mirror
(7) Forme: bench with no backrest
(8) Bellmettle: Bell metal – copper/tin alloy, greater tin content than in bronze
(9) Andirons: metal stand, usually in pairs, to support wood burning in a fireplace
(10) Scimer/scumer: device for skimming cream from milk
(11) Flitch of bacon: a side of bacon
(12) Scillet/skillet: small metal cooking pot with long handle and (usually) short legs
(13) Cobbirons: cobirons – pair of supports for a roasting spit
(14) Chafindish: chafing dish – cooking pot with outer pan of hot water to keep food hot
(15) Kneding trofe: kneading trough
(16) Kimnell/kymnell: wooden trough used (eg) for kneading dough
(17) Cheespres: cupboard for storing (eg) chesse
(18) Powderin tub/trof: powdering tub/trough – a tub/trough for salting or curing meat in
(19) Potshelle: a used pot, probably broken
(20) Wheells: in the context used here, most probably spinning wheels

Appendix 5
Will of Allen Hurrell of Newton, 1698

In the Name of God Amen, I Allen Hurrell of Newton in the County of Cambridge,
Yeoman, doe make this my last will and Testament touching
my temporall estate as followeth, first I give & bequeath all my freehold landes and
Tenements with th(e) app(ur)ten(an)ces lying & being within the feilds of Newton
aforesaid Hauxton & Harston in the said county which I lately purchased of
William Etheridge and Mary his wife, unto Anne my loving wife for
& during her naturall life, in lieu of dower & thirds, & from & after the death of my
said wife I doe give & bequeath the said lands and Tenements
with th(e) app(ur)ten(an)ces unto my daughter Sarah Hurrell and her heires. Item I
give and bequeath unto my sonn William Hurrell & his heires All those my
freehold lands with th(e) app(ur)ten(an)ces lying in Harston aforesaid containing by
estimacon one & twenty acres be the same more or less which
were given & devised to me & my heires by my brother in law John Greenell gent
deceased. Item I give to my sonn William Hurrell
ffive Hundred pounds of lawfull money of England to be paid within one yeare after my
decease. Item I give & bequeath unto my daughter
Elizabeth Hurrell the sume Two Hundred pounds of lawfull money of England to be
paid within six months after my decease. Item I give
& bequeath unto my daughter Susann the sume of fifty pounds of like money of England
to be paid within one yeare after my decease. Item I give & bequeath unto the said
Anne my wife one wrought bed in the Hall Chamber with the Curtaines, valisure &
bedstead bedding chaires chaires & stooles the suite belonging.
Item I give & bequeath unto my said wife All that mesuage or Tenement which I hold
of the Master, ffellowes & Schollars of St Peters Colledge in
the University of Cambridge, which I had by the gift & bequest of my sister Martha
Hawkes late of Cambridge aforesaid widow deceased
now in the occupacon of Mr Abraham Baker situate lying & being in little St Maries
parish in Cambridge aforesaid for & during the terme of
her naturall life She paying the Colledge rent as it shall become due for the same & after
her decease I give the said mesuage or tenement unto my
two sons Allen Hurrell & William Hurrell their heires and Assignes for ever. Item I give
& bequeath unto my said daughters Elizabeth
and Sarah All those my Three mesuages or Tenements which were lately given & devised
to me in & by the last will & Testament of my said
sister Martha Hawkes which I hold of the Master ffellowes & Schollars of Bennet
Colledge in the University of Cambridge aforesaid now

Will of Allen Hurrell of Newton, 1698

in the occupacon of Mr Walton Mr Williams & Mr Shippey situate lying & being in	
the parish of St Bennet in Cambridge aforesaid for &	19
during the terme of their naturall lives & after or either of decease then I give the said	
three messuages or tenements to the heires of them or	20
either of them lawfully to be begotten, And if it shall happen that the said Elizabeth &	
Sarah shall depart this life without heires of their	21
or either of their bodies so lawfull begotten then I give the said three messuages or	
tenements unto my said sonn Allen Hurrell his	22
heires & Assignes for ever And my mind & will is that my said daughters shall pay	
unto Elizabeth Watson of Cambridge aforesaid widow	23
the sume of foure pounds of lawful money of England yearely & every yeare during her	
naturall life to be paid quarterly at twenty shillings	24
a quarter by the said Elizabeth and Sarah. Item I give unto my sonn Allen Hurrell All my	
copyhold lands & tenements lying in the town & feilds of Newton Hauxton &	25
Harston aforesaid. Item I give and bequeath unto the foure Children of my daughter	
Jane Jron^(*), that is to say Allen Jron, John Jron, Joseph Jron	26
& Robert Jron twenty pounds apiece to be paid unto them when they shall attain to	
their severall & respective ages of one and twenty	27
yeares. Item I give unto the poor of the parish of Newton aforesaid twenty shillings.	
Item I give and bequeath unto my said wife five pounds	28
to buy her mourning, All the rest of my goods Chattells & personall estate after my	
debts legacies and funerall Charges paid I give &	29
bequeath unto my said sons Allen Hurrell and William Hurrell whome I doe make &	
appoint sole Executors of this my last & testam(en)t	30
in witness whereof I have hereunto set my hand & seale the third day of ffebruary in the	
fourth yeare of the Raigne of our Soveraigne	31
Lord William the third by the grace of God of England Scotland ffrance & Ireland	
King Defender of the faith [?] Anno[q?] Dm 1698	32

Signed Sealed & published & Declared by the   Memorand(um) that ye words "the sume of fifty
said Allen Hurrell the Testator & for   Pounds" "same", "three" "yeare" "life" "by ye said
the last will & Testament in the pre^{ce} (of) foure   Elizabeth & Sarah" were int(er)lined before
of us whose names are hereto subscribed   sealing hereof

James: Fletcher   the marke of
Thomas Pitts   Allen   Hurrell
Jos: Eyk

                                                                    Probate granted 7 Dec 1700/
                                                                    Allen Hurrell & [Wm(?)] Hurrell
                                                                        G Cooke (signed)

(*) (Line 26) The surname Jron should be Jon: Erasmus Jon married Jane Hurrell on the 16 Nov 1685, Royston, the 4 children were born in Sawston and Chesterton, Camb.

General comment: Words in *[italics]* are difficult to transcribe accurately.

Appendix 6
Inventory of Goods and Chattels of Allen Hurrell of Newton, 1700

	£	s	d	Line
A True and P[er]fect Inventory of all ye Goods and				1
Chattels of Allen Hurrell of Newton in ye County				2
of Cambridge Yeoman taken and apprised by us				3
whose names are underwritten this fifteenth				4
day of October 1700				6
				7
Impriss for his wareing Apparill and money in his purs - -	20	00	00	8
Itim in y^e Hall Chamber one bed with beding and Chaires				9
belongeing to itt with other Lumber - - - -	9	10	00	10
Itim in y^e Littill Chamber over y^e Sillir$^{(1)}$ one bed with				11
Chaires belongeing to itt with other Lumber - - -	6	00	00	12
Itim in y^e Parlar Chamber three beds with other				13
Lumber - - - - - - -	10	00	00	14
Itim y^e Maids Chamber one bed - - - - -	1	00	00	15
Itim in y^e Garrett ould Lumber - - - -	1	05	00	16
Itim in y^e Parlar one Clock two tables 13 Chaires				17
one Lookinglas with other Lumber - - -	6	10	00	18
Itim in y^e Hall 3 tables 11 Chaires with other Lumber - -	2	13	00	19
Itim in y^e Kitchin one Jack$^{(2)}$ with Chaires and other Lumber -	2	05	06	20
Itim for Poulter$^{(3)}$ - - - - - -	4	15	04	21
Itim for bras Coppers$^{(4)}$ and bruing vesils - - - -	8	03	04	22
Itim in y^e Dary one Chesepres$^{(5)}$ and Churn with other Lumber -	2	03	00	23
Itim for a parsell$^{(6)}$ of Cheses - - - -	5	00	00	24
Itim for a boughtin mill$^{(7)}$ with other Lumber - -	1	00	00	25
Itim for 3 flockbeads$^{(8)}$ in y^e Searvants Chamber - -	1	10	00	26
Itim in y^e Sillirs hogsheads and barrils with				27
other Lumber - - - - - -	3	04	00	28
Itim for Sheets and napkins and other wareing linin - -	9	10	00	29
Itim for one Sillver Tankard - - - - -	6	10	00	30
Itim for 40 hogs and pigs - - - - -	20	18	08	31
Itim for 21 Cowes and a bull - - - -	51	06	08	32
Itim for a parsell of wooll - - - -	20	00	00	33
Itim for nine horses and there harneses - - -	78	15	00	34
Itim for one wagon and four carts - - - -	20	00	00	35
Itim for plowes harrows and rouls$^{(9)}$ with other Lumber - -	4	00	00	36
Itim for sacks and screen$^{(10)}$ and bushel$^{(11)}$ with other				37
Lumber - - - - - - - -	3	10	00	38

Inventory of Goods and Chattels of Allen Hurrell of Newton, 1700

	£	s	d	
Itim for a parsell of hay - - - - - -	11	00	00	39
Itim for a parsell of Lintills[12] in y^e Straw - - - - -	13	00	00	40
Itim for a parsell of peares[13] in Straw - - - - -	30	00	00	41
Itim for a parsell of rie and wheat in ye Garner[14] - - - -	4	10	00	42
Itim for a parsell of ots and wheat in ye Straw - - - -	3	04	00	43
Itim for fifteen score and nine Sheep - - - - -	103	05	00	44
Itim for plowing 50 acers of tylth 4 times - - - -	28	09	04	45
Itim for 14 quarters[15] of wheat to sow itt - - - -	21	00	00	46
Itim for 26 acers plowing three times - - - -	11	01	00	47
Itim for nine quarters of mesline[16] to sow itt - - -	9	00	00	48
Itim for plowing of sixty acers of tylth				49
twise - - - - - - - - -	17	00	00	50
Itim for Carridg of dung and mud - - - - -	5	00	00	51
Itim for plowing 20 acers of Stubble - - - - -	3	00	00	52
Itim for barly in ye Straw - - - - - -	221	00	00	53
Itim for mesline in ye Straw - - - - - -	50	00	00	54
Itim for wheat in ye Straw - - - - - -	77	00	00	55
Itim for dects[17] good and Desperett[18] - - - -	250	00	00	56

(Signed)	Will Stevenson	57
	John Sargeant	58

Notes:

1. Sillir – probably Cellar
2. Jack – device for turning the spit when roasting meat over a fire
3. Poulter – pewter; presumably a large pot made thereof
4. Coppers – large cauldron
5. Chesepres – cheese press: cupboard for storing cheese
6. parsell – parcel: a quantity of things
7. boughtin mill – probably boulting mill: sieve used to separate flour from bran
8. flockbeads – flockbeds: flock filled mattresses
9. rouls – probably rollers used to break up soil
10. screen – a (large) sieve
11. bushel – in the context, probably a vessel used as a bushel measure
12. Lintills – probably lentils; "in ye Straw": unthreshed
13. peares – pears (consistent with inventory date: mid-October)
14. Garner – (grain) store
15. quarters – quantity: usually 8 bushels of grain
16. mesline – maslin: mixture of wheat and rye; either grown together or mixed later
17. dects – in the context, most probably debts
18. Desperett – desparate: debts not recoverable (from late Middle English)

Appendix 7

Wills Referred to in this History

PRO: Public Record Office
CRO: Cambridge Record Office
ERO: Essex Record Office

Roger Hurrell of Sible Hedingham, Probate 1540, ERO Catalogue Reference D/ABW 18/78, 1 page.

Willam Hurrell of Warners, Sible Hedingham, Probate 1593, ERO Catalogue Reference D/ABW 19/235, 1 page.

George Hurrell of Sible Hedingham, Probate 1610, ERO Catalogue Reference D/ABW 20/146, 4 pages.

Thomas Hurrell of Sible Hedingham, Probate 1613, ERO Catalogue Reference D/ABW 20/214, 1 pages. (Nuncupative will).

John Hurrell of Sible Hedingham, Probate 1616, ERO Catalogue Reference D/ABW 20/284, 1 pages. (Nuncupative will).

Allin Hurrell of Bourne, Probate 1623, PRO Catalogue Reference: Prob 11/142, Image Reference: 252, 2 pages.

Allen Hurrell of Harston, Probate 1650, PRO Catalogue Reference: Prob 11/215, Image Reference: 566, 1 page.

Elizabeth Hurrell of Harston, Probate 1671, CRO Reference VC 31:176 1671 CW In, 2 pages and inventory.

Annabel Hurrell of Foxton, Probate 1686, CRO Reference VC 34:65 1686 CW In, 1 page and inventory.

Wills Referred to in this History

Martha Hawkes of Cambridge, Probate 1698, 1 page.

John Greenhill of Sawston, Probate 1677, PRO Catalogue Reference: Prob 11/356, Image Reference: 141, 3 pages.

Allen Hurrell of Newton, Probate 1700, CRO Reference VC 35:512 1700 CW In,

Allen Hurrell of Harston, Probate 1740 CRO Reference VC 40:258 1740 CW, 2 pages.

John Hamilton Mortimer, Probate 1779, 1 page.

William Hurrell of Newton, Probate 1781, PRO Catalogue Reference: Prob 11/1074, Image reference: 237, 4 pages.

Thomas Hurrell of Chishill Hall, Probate 1816, PRO Catalogue Reference: Prob 11/1582, Image Reference: 223, 2 pages.

William Stacey Hurrell of Foxton, Probate 1836, PRO Catalogue Reference: Prob 11/1868, Image Reference: 63 & 64, 8 pages.

Martha Hurrell of Foxton, Probate 1845, Pro Ctalogue Reference: Prob 11/2010, Image Reference: 295, 3 pages.

John Pottrell of Littlebury Green, Probate 1779.

Rebecca Hurrell of Orwell, Probate 1801, PRO Catalogue Reference: Prob 11/1360, Image Reference: 208, 2 pages.

Allen Hurrell of Arkesden, Probate 1838, PRO Catalogue Reference: Prob 11/1902, 5 pages.

Appendix 8

Census Records Referred to in this History

PRO: Public Record Office

1841 Census

Elizabeth White, (with Hannah White, grandmother), Cricklade.
Parish: Wanborough.
PRO Reference: HO107 piece 1179 folio 12/27 page 1.

Joseph Head, (with Honour and Maria), 'Near the Pond'.
Parish: East Ilsley.
PRO Reference: HO107 piece 14 folio 6/4 page 3

Lucy Hurrell & Family, Farmer, Hobs Aire.
Parish: Arkesden.
PRO Reference: HO107 piece 340 folio 13 page 20

1851 Census

Emma Wait, (with Simon Etty), House Servant, Cricklade.
Parish: Wanborough.
PRO Reference: HO107 piece 1833 folio 329 page 22

Elizabeth, Jane, Fanny & Maria Hurrell, Visitors, 13 Salisbury Place.
Parish: Marylebone.
PRO Reference: HO107 piece 1489 folio 20 page 31/32

Lucy Toplis, (dau.-in-law with James Toplis), 43 Bernard Street, Finsbury.
Parish: St George, Bloomsbury.
PRO Reference: HO107 piece 1507 folio 102 page 18

William Hurrell, (Brother-in-law with Henry Toplis), Brewer's Collector, 8 Frederick Street, Marylebone.
Parish: St Pancras.
PRO Reference: HO107 piece 1493 folio 251 page 63

1861 Census

Honor Head, Formally Shopkeeper, Compton Road.
Parish: East Ilsley.
PRO Reference: RG09 piece 737 folio 133 page 19

William Hurrell & Family, Beer Seller, 21 College Place, Marylebone.
Parish: St Pancras.
PRO Reference: RG09 piece 116 folio 68 page 58

1871 Census

Honor Head (with Charles Stanton, Coachman), The Lodge, Williamscott Hamlet, Cropredy Village.
Parish: Cropredy.
PRO Reference: RG10 piece 1463 folio 110 page 3 & 4

William Hurrell & Family, Traveller, 21 College Place, Marylebone.
Parish: St Pancras.
PRO Reference: RG10 piece 232 folio 104 page 47

1881 Census

Honour Head (with Charles Stanton, Coachman Domestic Servant), Williamscott Hamlet.
Parish: Wardington.
PRO Reference: RG11 piece 1530 folio 34 page 12

Elizabeth Hurrell, Licensed Victualler, The George & Dragon.
Parish: Wandsworth.
PRO Reference: RG11 piece 657 folio 40 page 12

John Byles, Clerk idle, (boarder with Harry Cole), 24 G Street, Hans Town.
Parish: Chelsea.
PRO Reference: RG11 piece 90 folio 10 page 13

Appendix 8

1891 Census

Elizabeth A Dunn (& family), 43 Waldemar Avenue, London.
Parish: Fulham.
PRO Reference: RG12 piece 54 folio 59 page 19

Elizabeth Hurrell, (& Henry A C) Licensed Victualler, 14 West Hill Road, (George & Dragon).
Parish: Wandsworth.
PRO Reference: RG12 piece 445 folio 87 page 34

William Hurrell (The Major) & Florence, Living on own means, 34 Hugh Street, London.
Parish: St George Hanover Square.
PRO Reference: RG12 piece 73 folio 65 page 10

1901 Census

Henry A C Hurrell (& Edith), Licensed Victualler, 14 West Hill Road (George & Dragon).
Parish: Wandsworth.
PRO Reference: RG13 piece 481 folio 107 page 3

Lucy Toplis, Living on own means, 28 Southampton Road.
Parish: St Pancras.
PRO Reference: RG13 piece 154 folio 13 page 17

Appendix 9

Documents in Relation to the Case in Chancery of Toplis v Hurrell

(18 April 1850 to 12 June 1856)

C14/1186/T37 18 April 1850

Bill of Complaint of Henry John Fuller Toplis and Lucy his wife and Others, and Answers of the Defendants William Hurrell, Charles Rider and John Cater Canning.

17 November 1851

Between
Henry John Fuller Toplis and Lucy his wife, Elizabeth Hurrell, Allen Hurrell, William Hurrell, Jane Hurrell, Fanny Hurrell and Maria Hurrell, plaintiffs
And
William Hurrell, Charles Rider, John Cater Canning and James Toplis the Younger, defendants.

The Plaintiffs in this Cause join issue with the Defendants

Deposition of John Cater Canning 3 July 1854
Deposition of Wyatt Given Gibson a partner in Gibson & co, 3 July 1854
Depositions of John Dobede Taylor, solicitor, 13 Jan 1855 and 3 Feb 1855
Deposition of Elizabeth Hurrell, 10 Feb 1855
Deposition of Jane Hurrell, 3 March 1855
Deposition of Fanny Hurrell, 23 Feb 1855
Deposition of Lucy Toplis, 23 Feb 1855

Deposition of Allen Hurrell, 1 March 1855
Deposition of William Hurrell, plaintiff, 12 March 1855
Deposition of Charles Rider, 16 April 1855
Deposition of William Hurrell, defendant, 13 April 1855
Deposition of Joseph Francis, bailiff of the farm after the death of Allen Hurrell, 23 May 1855

C38/2230

Masters Reports 2 March 1853

Between Henry John Fuller Toplis and Lucy his wife, Elizabeth Hurrell, Allen Hurrell, William Hurrell, Jane Hurrell, Fanny Hurrell and Augustin King George and Maria Hurrell
Plaintiffs
And
William Hurrell, Charles Rider, John Cater Canning and James Toplis the Younger,
Defendants

A draft of Interrogatories was prepared and exhibited for the examination of the Defendant John Cater Canning.

Deposition of John Cater Canning 3 July 1854.

C38/2260

Masters Reports 27 July 1854

Between Henry John Fuller Toplis and Lucy his wife, Elizabeth Hurrell, Allen Hurrell, William Hurrell, Jane Hurrell, Fanny Hurrell and Augustin King George and Maria Hurrell
Plaintiffs
And
William Hurrell, Charles Rider, John Cater Canning and James Toplis the Younger,
Defendants

The Plaintiffs and Defendants (except the Defendant John Cater Canning) have attended by their respective Solicitors. The said Defendant John Cater Canning has not attended although duly summoned.

Monies paid and allowed and Affidavits.

C38/2302
Masters Reports 15 November 1855

Between Henry John Fuller Toplis and Lucy his wife, Elizabeth Hurrell, Allen Hurrell, William Hurrell, Jane Hurrell, Fanny Hurrell, Augustin King George and Maria his wife late Maria Hurrell
Plaintiffs
And
William Hurrell, Charles Rider, John Cater Canning and James Toplis the younger
Defendants

Summarising details of the children, receipts and disbursements, debts, funeral expenses, legacies, residuary real estate and value of the sale of the Testators real estate.

C33/1038, f. 497
Decrees and Orders 11 February 1856

Between Henry John Fuller Toplis and Lucy his wife, Elizabeth Hurrell, Allen Hurrell, William Hurrell, Jane Hurrell, Fanny Hurrell, and Augustin King George and Maria his wife, late Maria Hurrell
Plaintiffs
William Hurrell, Charles Rider, John Cater Canning and James Toplis the Younger, since deceased.
Defendants
And Between the same Plaintiffs and
Edward Toplis, Defendant

The causes are transferred from the Book of Causes of the Right Honourable the Master of the Rolls to that of the Right Honourable the Lords Justices.

C33/1039, f. 1026
Decrees and Orders 8 May 1856

Between Henry John Fuller Toplis and Lucy his wife, Elizabeth Hurrell, Allen Hurrell, William Hurrell, Jane Hurrell, Fanny Hurrell, and Augustin King George and Maria his wife, late Maria Hurrell
Plaintiffs
William Hurrell, Charles Rider, John Cater Canning and James Toplis the Younger, since deceased.
Defendants
And Between the same Plaintiffs and
Edward Toplis, Defendant

The court orders each of the Defendants William Hurrell and Charles Rider on or before the 9th day of June 1856 to pay the sum of £500 into the Bank with the privity of the Accountant General of the Court.

C33/1039, ff. 1316-17
Decrees and Orders 12 June 1856

Between Henry John Fuller Toplis and Lucy his wife Elizabeth Hurrell Allen Hurrell William Hurrell Jane Hurrell Fanny Hurrell and Augustin King George and Maria his wife late Maria Hurrell
Plaintiffs
William Hurrell, Charles Rider, John Cater Canning and James Toplis the Younger since deceased
Defendants
And between the same Plaintiffs and Edward Toplis, Defendant.

Hearings before Counsel for the Defendants William Hurrell and Charles Rider but no one appeared for John Cater Canning.

Ordered that John Cater Canning do on or before 15 July 1856 or within 7 days after service upon him of the Order pay into the Bank with the privity of the Accountant General the sum of £2982-14-3.

Settlement of the money to be paid out to the Plaintiffs.

Bibliography

Books and Periodicals

Alderman, Geoffrey, *Modern Britain 1700—1983*, Croom Helm Ltd, 1986.

Aylmer, G.E., *Rebellion or Revolution? England from Civil War to Restoration*, Oxford University Press, 1987.

Bedarida, Francois, *A Social History of England 1851—1975, translated by A.S. Forster*, Methuen & Co Ltd, 1979.

Blanning, T.C.W., Ed., *Oxford Illustrated History of Modern Europe*, Oxford, 1996.

Burke, *The General Armory, page 522*, 1878.

Dudley, Geoffrey A., *The Yeoman of England*, Family Tree Magazine, December 1986.

Ensor, Robert, *The Oxford History of England: England 1870—1914, 2nd Edition*, Oxford Clarendon Press, 1974.

Overton, Mark, *Agricultural Revolution in England: The Transformation of the Agrarian Economy 1500—1850*, Cambridge University Press, 1996.

Parker, Rowland, *The Common Stream*, William Collins Sons & Co Ltd, 1975.

Williams, Basil, *The Oxford History of England: The Whig Supremacy 1714—1760, 2nd Edition revised by C.H. Stuart*, Oxford Clarendon Press, 1974.

Woodward, Llewellyn, *The Oxford History of England: The Age of Reform 1815—1870, 2nd Edition*, Oxford Clarendon Press, 1974.

Bibliography

Online

British History Online: Parishes of Harston, Foxton, Hauxton and Newton.

Essex Archives Online: Enclosure of the common fields in Arkesden and Wendens Ambo parishes.

Wikipedia: The free Internet encyclopedia.

The Victorian Web Online: Literature, history and culture in the age of Victoria.

The National Archives: Documents online—entries for Domesday Book, Arkesden and Foxton.

Index of Places

This index is organised by country and county. Places are only included if they are relevant to the Hurrell story. Spellings in some documents quoted in this book may differ from those below.

Australia
  New South Wales
    - Orange 78
    - Sydney 127

England

Berkshire 81, 83
  East Ilsley 82, 144, 145
  Ilsley 82,
  Wantage 82, 83

Buckinghamshire
  High Wycombe 34

Cambridgeshire vii, 16, 43, 69, 71, 106, 115
  Bourn/Bourne ix, 1, 5, 9, 12, 15, 16, 142
  Cambridge vii, 4, 7, 9, 12, 40, 44, 45, 47, 71, 143
    - Benet College 22, 138
    - Bridge St. 40
    - Jesus College 25
    - Market Hill 40
    - St Mary the Great 21, 138
    - St Michael's 18
    - St Peter's College 22, 138
  Croxton 27
  Ely 22
    - Consistory Court 43
    - Diocese of 43
    - Dean and Chapter 50
  Fowlmere 49
  Foxton vii, viii, 1, 3, 5, 11, 16, 17, 18, 19, 22, 28, 29, 31, 34, 35, 37, 38, 39, 40, 43, 44, 45, 46, 51, 58, 71, 72, 87, 115, 142, 143
    - Bendyshe estate 43
    - Bury estate 18, 43
    - Chancel, Foxton Church 42
    - Foxton Bury 31, 37, 40, 43, 45, 49, 51
    - Foxton Hall 3, 47, 51
    - Foxton House 46, 50, 51
    - Hatton Estate 43
    - Malting House 49
    - Mortimer Lane 11
    - Mortimer's (barn) 18
  Gamlingay 27
  Harston vii, viii, 1, 3, 5, 16, 19, 21, 22, 25, 27, 29, 31, 34, 43, 77, 106, 115, 142, 143
    - Harston Hall 3
    - Park House vii, 39, 77
    - the Swann 28
  Hauxton 21, 22
    - Ely manor 25
  Littlebury Green 53, 58, 143
  Little Shelford 40
  Madingley Hall 4, 69
  Melbourn 47, 49, 69
  Newton viii, 1, 3, 4, 5, 18, 19, 21, 22, 25, 31, 32, 34, 35, 37, 43, 44, 51, 58, 106, 115, 143
    - Manor Farm 67, 69
    - Newton Bury 22, 37, 43
    - Newton Hall 3
  Orwell 45, 143
  Royston Park 5
  Sawston ix, 1, 5, 7, 9, 10, 16, 18, 21, 27, 40, 42, 143
    - Brooke House 27
    - Sawston Mills 40
    - The White Hart 10
  Trumpington 37, 43
  Witcham 39

Derbyshire
  Snitterton Hall 104

Essex
  Arkesden vii, ix, 4, 5, 40, 54, 55, 57, 58, 59, 63, 66, 69, 70, 71, 72,,74, 76, 78, 79, 87, 98, 117, 125, 129, 130, 143
    - Arkesden Church 42, 78, 79, 128
    - Becketts 60, 65, 67, 70, 78, 98
    - Clodmorehill 57
    - Hobs Aerie (Hobsary) 4, 53, 54, 55, 57, 58, 59, 60, 65, 67, 74, 77, 78, 98, 117, 144
    - Peverells/Peverils 53, 54, 55, 58
  Boreham viii, 115
  Bulmer viii, 115
    - Brundon Hall viii, 115
  Castle Hedingham 111, 114
    - St. Nicholas Church 114
  Chelmsford (Essex Record Office) 109, 118
    - Chelmsford Chronicle 73
  Chrishall 45, 53
    - Chrishall Hall 40, 143
  Elmdon 28, 31, 57

Index of Places

Elsenham 58
Great Maplestead 110
Halstead 7, 9, 10, 111
Haverhill 7
Havering Attic Bower 13
Lamarsh 8, 111, 112, 113
Littlebury 53, 57
  - Littlebury Green 53
Little Maplestead 116
  - Hurrell's Farm 116
Malden Heybridge viii, 115
Maplestead viii
Newport 71, 72
Quendon 118, 120, 121, 122
  - Quendon Hall 55, 117, 118, 120
Saffron Walden 57
Sible Hedingham (Himingham) vii, viii, ix, x, 1, 5, 7,
    8, 9, 10, 11, 12, 13, 15, 16, 17, 109, 110, 111,
    113, 114, 115, 142
  - Aldersford Almshouse 110
  - Aldersford Street 9
  - Barnard's/Bernard's Farm 109, 110, 116
  - Bloyes/Blois Hall 110, 111, 115
  - Highsted Grene (Green) 10
  - Huntis/Huntes 112
  - Hurrontes 110, 111
  - Mekitoes 10, 11, 17
  - Potters Street 17
  - St Peter's Church 7, 114
  - Warners 8, 110, 111, 112
  - Warrens 111, 116
Stisted 111
Stambourne 113
Stansted 78
Toppesfield
  - Hurall's Farm 116
Wendon Lofts 57
Wendens Ambo 55

Gloucestershire
  Cheltenham 38

Hampshire
  Stratton Pk, Micheldever 98

Hertfordshire
  Bishop's Stortford 58, 67, 68, 70
    - Public Library 121
    - Taylor & Collinson 70
    - Taylor & Fairman, Solicitors 70
  Brocket Hall 34
  Hitchin 50

Royston 28, 48, 49, 50
St. Albans 122

Kent
  Hartley, Dartford vii
  Dover 81, 83

Lancashire
  Liverpool
    - Ashgrove, Wavertree 94

Leicestershire
  Bardon 133

Linconshire
  Syston 98

London
  General, including parts of Middlesex and Surrey 38,
    44, 51, 59
  Battersea
    - St Mark's Church 95
  Bloomsbury 70
    - St George 144
  Camden Town 77, 81, 83, 87, 90, 98, 118, 145
    - Camden High Street 87, 88
    - Camden Library 90
    - College Place 77, 81, 83, 86, 88, 145
    - North London Collegiate (School) vii, 87, 88, 90
    - North London Collegiate Sch. for Girls 87, 89
  Chancery (Court/case) ix, 4, 22, 34, 54, 55, 59, 65,
    66, 70, 72, 77, 118
  Chelsea
    - Hans Town 94, 145
  Clerkenwell
    - St John the Baptist 86
  Ealing 133
  Enfield 57
  Frederick St, Hampstead Rd. 57, 67, 68, 70, 71, 72,
    117, 145
  Fulham
    - St James Ch. 94
    - Waldemar Avenue 95, 146
  Grovenor Square
    - Gilbert St. 103
  Hackney 121, 122
  Harrow 87
  Islington
    - St Mary's Church, 55
  Kensal Green Cemetery 78, 130
  Kings Bench 120, 121
  Leytenstone 125

Index of Places

Marylebone
- Charlotte St 86
- Salisbury Place 70, 144

Newgate 122

Paddington 79

Pimlico
- Denbigh St 98
- St Saviours 98
- Hugh St 98, 146

Poplar 78, 129

Putney
- Alec Binnie Studio 93, 103

Royal Academy 32

Shadwell 125

St Clement Dane's Church 34

St Georges, Hanover Square 57

St Pancras 57, 70, 77, 81
- Parish of Old St. Pancras 86
- Highgate Rd. 90
- St John's Church 86
- St Matthew's Ch. Oakley Sq. 94
- Southampton Rd. 77, 146
- Southampton Terrace 77
- Willow Walk 90

St Paul's Churchyard 57, 67

St Paul's Church, Covent Garden 32

St Saviour's Church, Maida Vale 57

Twickenham
- Orlean's House Estate 34
- Ragman's Castle, 34
- Riverside 34

Wandsworth viii, ix, 82, 90, 96, 103
- Cemetery 95, 103, 105
- Earl Spencer, Merton Rd. 105
- Garrett Lane Old Burial Ground 93
- George and Dragon ix, 82, 93, 94, 95, 101, 103, 104, 105, 145, 146
- Lebanon Terrace, West Hill 95
- West Hill 93, 103
- Ye Olde Bull 93, 105
- Young's Brewery 93

Westminster 128
- St Clement Danes 34

Monmouthshire
Newport 72

Northamptonshire
Wakefield Lodge, Passenham 98

Newcastle
North Shields viii

Oxfordshire 83
Williamscote 82, 145

Somerset
Bath 38

Suffolk
Stoke-juxta-Clare 13
Sudbury 115

Surrey
Guildford 128

Sussex
Brighton 57, 77, 78, 79, 130
- St Mary,s Church 130
- Sussex Square 57
Eastbourne 32, 34
Hastings 78, 103
- Holy Trinity Church 103
- Imperial Hotel 95
St Leonards-on-Sea 95

Warwickshire
Leamington 47
West Bromwich 48
- All Saints Church 47

Wiltshire
Salisbury Cathedral 32
Wanborough 82, 83, 144

Yorkshire
Harrogate 38

France
Boulogne-sur-Mer 69
- Rue Neuve Chaussee 69
Caen 131
Douai Communal Cemetery 133
Marseilles 133

India
Bengal 118, 133
Bombay 40

New Zealand 40

Rhodesia (Zimbabwe) ix, 42, 100, 101, 106
Arkesden Farm, 100
Fort Victoria (Masvingo) 100

Foxton, Hunter's Road 101
Gwelo (Gweru) 3, 95, 100, 101, 105
Horseshoe Hotel 101, 104, 105
Harston (Farm), Zaloba Siding 3, 101, 105
Hunters Road 101
Limpopo river 100
Mashona 101
Matabele 100, 101
Salisbury (Harare) 4, 100
Zambesi River 100

South Africa 90, 91, 100
  Barberton 97
  Cape Town 95
  Eastern Transvaal (Mpumalanga) 97
  George 95
  Gaika and Zulu wars 91
    - Pilgrim's Rest 97
    - Zululand 95
  Hlobane Mountain 96
  Isandlwana 96
  Johannesburg 100
  Kambula 97
  Rorkes Drift 96
  Zlobanne Mountain 96

Index of People

Names in **bold type** are the direct line from George and Agnes Hurrell/Ann to the descendants of William Hurrell and Elizabeth Head.

Names of Hurrells and their spouses, mainly from Sibl Hedingham, whose relationship to George Hurrell and h descendants has yet to be established, are in a separat section at the end of this index.

Abbess of Charteris 37
Alderman
  Geoffrey 44
Asplen
  William Ward 50, 51
  Mary 50, 51
Bagally
  Mr (of the Chancery Court) 75
Bailey
  Mary 57, 58, 70, 78, 125, 129
Barnes
  J. B. 54
Bayles
  Ethel Annie (née Dunn) 134, 135
  John Charles 135
Beagg
  Joane 111
Bendyshe
  (Family) 37, 46
Biatt
  Jane 21
Binnie
  Alec (Photo Studio) 93, 103
Bone
  Lesley Kerr viii, ix, x, 117
  Philippa (née de Clancy Walsh) vii, viii, 4
Braybrooke
  Lord 40
Bridge
  John Littell (d. 1776) 25
  Margaret (née Hurrell) 25
Browne
  Dr Henry 70
  Robert 12
Buller
  Colonel 96
Butler
  Elizabeth (b. 1869, née Hurrell) 128
  Harold Herbert Fry 128

Index of People

Byles
    Elizabeth Ann (b. 1859, née Hurrell) x, 81, 82, 83, 90, 94, 95, 134
    Florence Annie 94, 95, 134, 135
    John 94, 134, 145
Cairns
    Mr (of the Chancery Court) 75
Canning
    George 58, 118, 122
    John Cater 4, 58, 63, 65, 66, 67, 68, 69, 70, 72, 73, 75, 76, 77, 121, 147, 148. 149
    Maria (née Gordon) 58, 118, 121, 122
    Thomas 58,
Cavendish
    Theodosia 47, 48
Cobden
    Richard (M.P.) 88, 89
Colenbrander
    Colonel 104
Collinson
    Mary 98
Cole
    Harry 94
Cooper
    Alfred William 133
    Florence Churchill 133
    Gladys Marion Millicent (née George) 133
Corder-Birch
    Adrian 110, 115
Cornings
    Richard 48
Cranmer
    Ethel Annie Worthington 57, 78, 79, 130
    Fanny (née Hurrell) 57, 59, 69, 70, 73, 76, 78, 79, 130
    George Archibald 57, 78, 130
    Henry 55, 117, 118 120, 121
    James Stewart Gordon 55, 86
    Martha 120
    Margaret 121
    (Rev) Robert 120
Cranmer Gordon
    Henry 117, 118
    James Stewart 117
    John 118
    Joseph (Jnr) 118, 120, 121
    Joseph (Snr) 55, 117, 118 120, 121, 122
    Lucy (c1765-1848, née unk'n) 57, 117, 118, 120, 122
    Richard 118, 121
    William 118
Curry
    Jane 114
Davis
    Elizabeth (Beth) (née Irvine, formerly Jackson) ix

    Martin ix
Dearsley
    Alice 105
    Eleanor 105
    Georgina 105
    Mary (née Collinson) 98
    David George 98
    Florence Annie 98, 100, 104, 105
Dinnis
    Francis Henry 86
Dunn
    Elizabeth Ann (b.1859, née Hurrell) x, 81, 82, 83, 90, 94, 95, 134, 146
    Ethel Annie 94, 95, 134, 135,
    William Nicholls 94, 95, 134
Edwards
    Thomas 121, 122
Etheridge
    Mary 21, 138
    William 21, 138
Etty
    (Rev) Simeon James 83
Everard
    Lucy Newland 133
Everett
    Alma 135
Field
    Edith (née Stone/Hurrell) 105, 106
    James 105, 106, 107
    Mr (Chancery Court) 75
Finch
    Catherine Frances 40, 42
    Charles 40
Fitzpatrick
    Sir Percy 97
Francis
    Joseph 73, 148
Garner
    James 49
    Naomi 49
Gatwood
    (First name unknown) 31
    Elizabeth (née Hurrell) 31, 34
Gee
    Mr (Attorney) 121, 122
George
    Arthur 133
    Augustin King 57, 72, 76, 77, 79, 133, 148, 149
    Duncan (b. 1856) 133
    Florence Churchill (née Cooper) 133
    Gladys Marion Millicent 133
    Herbert Duncan King (b. 1897) 133
    Lucy Newland (née Everard) 133

Index of People

Maria (b. 1827, née Hurrell) 57, 72, 76, 78, 79, 133, 148, 149
Gibson
  Anne (née Hurrell) 40
  (Rev) John Dawson 40
  Wyatt Given 72, 147
Giles
  Emma 90
  Harry 90
  Sophia 90
Gordon
  Lucy (1790-1849) 42, 55, 57, 58, 59, 65, 66, 67, 69, 76, 117, 118, 119, 125
  Maria 58, 118
Gordon Cranmer
  James Stewart (b. 1800) 57, 117, 118, 121, 122
Grafton
  Duke of 98
Greenhill
  Elizabeth (dau. of Henry) 18
  Frances (d. of Henry) 18
  Henry (Snr) 17, 18
  Henry (Jnr, s. of Henry) 18
  Jane (dau. of Henry) 18
  Jane/Jeane (wife of Allen Hurrell) 18, 21, 25
  Jane (née Biatt) 21
  John (d. 1677) 18, 21, 22, 138, 143
  Mary (b. 1642, née Hurrell) 17
  Mary (dau. of Henry) 18
  William 18
Grey
  Giles 111
Greygoose — see Winton
Hadden
  Edwin Alfred 95, 134
  Mary/Pollie (née Hurrell) 95, 134
Halcrow
  Clifford Haigh 134
  Florence Annie (née Byles) 134, 135
Hawkes
  Jacob 17
  Martha (née Hurrell) 17, 18, 22, 138
Hawles
  Margery 113
Head
  Elizabeth (born Wayte) viii, ix, 81, 82, 83, 86, 87, 89, 93, 95, 98, 103, 134
  Emma 82
  Honour/Honor (née Wayte) 82, 83, 145
  Joseph 82, 83, 86, 144
  Maria 82
  Mary Ann 82

Hunwick/Hunwicke/Hunicke
  Agnes 9
  Alane 9
  Allin 114
  Ellyn 114
  Francis 8, 9, 114
Hopkins
  Anne (née Hurrell) 28
  William 28, 31
Horn
  Gladys 105
Hurle
  William 13
Hurrell (General)
  Census records 144-146
  Wills 23, 24, 138-143
  Chancery Court (1850-56) 147-150
Hurrell
  Agnes (née Hunwick) 9
  Agnes (née Regan) 128
  Allen/Allin (1599-1650/1) 10, 16, 17, 142
  Allen (1635-1700) 17, 18, 21, 22, 25, 138, 139, 143
  Allen (c1660-1740) 21, 22, 25, 27, 29, 31, 138, 139, 143
  Allen (1689-1746) 25, 27, 29
  Allen (1741-1809) 34
  Allen (1768-1838) vii, 3, 40, 42, 45, 46, 53, 54, 55, 57, 58, 59, 66, 72, 73, 77, 79, 86, 117, 118, 119, 123, 143
  Allen (b.1803) 47, 48, 49, 72
  Allen (b.1817) 57, 58, 59, 63, 65, 67, 70, 73, 76, 78, 87, 98, 125, 129, 147, 148, 149
  Allen (b.1853) 78, 125
  Allen (b. 1882) 125
  Allen (b. 1886) 125
  Allin (b.1618) 114
  Allyn/Allin (c1559-1623) ix, 8, 9, 10, 11, 12, 13, 15, 16, 112, 114, 142
  Amelia Matilda (née Williams) 128
  Angela (née Nolan Mears) vii, viii, ix
  Annabel (1632-1685) 16, 17, 18, 51, 142
  Ann (bp. 1607, dau. of John Hurrell) 11
  Ann (c1535-1617) 8, 9, 10, 12
  Anne (née Smith) 31, 34
  Ann (1797-1842) 40, 46
  Ann (1819-1849) 57, 58, 59, 67, 68, 69, 73 76, 77
  Anna (née Webb) 22, 25, 27, 31
  Anne (née Stacey) 32, 37, 39, 42
  Anne (née unk'n) 21, 22
  Anne (1694-1771) 28, 29
  Anne (c1822-1850) 40
  Arthur (b.1874) 129
  Arthur James 125
  Bill Crawford 4

Index of People

Charles (NZ) 40
Catherine Frances (née Finch) 40, 42
Catherine (b. 1856) 78
Dale vii
Dave 101, 105
Dorothy/Dorothie (b.1562) 8, 11, 12, 112, 113
Edith Charlotte (née Stone) 103, 105, 106
Eliza 69
Elizabeth (dau of Allyn) 10, 11, 16
Elizabeth (née Head) viii, ix, 81, 82, 83, 86, 87, 89, 93, 95, 98, 101, 103, 104, 134, 145, 146
Elizabeth (née Swann) 22, 31
Elizabeth (née Thurgood) 9, 10, 12, 15, 16
Elizabeth (née unk'n d.1671) 16, 17, 136, 142
Elizabeth (b. c1665) 22, 138
Elizabeth (1699-1706) 27, 31
Elizabeth (1704-1770 née Hurrell) 27, 31, 34, 43
Elizabeth (b.1728) 31, 34
Elizabeth (1770-1857) 40, 42
Elizabeth (1800-1886) 47, 48, 49, 51, 57
Elizabeth (1815-1911) 57, 59, 67, 69, 70, 73, 76, 77, 78, 79, 144, 147, 148, 149
Elizabeth (b. 1869) 128
Elizabeth (b. 1889) 128
Elizabeth Ann (b. 1859) x, 81, 82, 83, 90, 94, 134
Elizabeth Annie 125
Elizabeth Matilda (née Smith) 125
Ellen (née Seekamp) 66, 69
Fanny (b.1826) 57, 59, 69, 70, 73, 76, 78, 79, 130, 144, 147, 148, 149
Florence Annie (née Dearsley) 100, 104, 105
Geoffrey Dearsley 77, 105
Geoffrey Taylor 77, 106
George (c1535-1610) ix, 8, 9, 10, 11, 12, 15, 17, 109, 111, 112, 113, 114, 115, 142
Grace 100, 105
Grace (b.1560) 113
Hannah (d.1807) 13
Henry (d. inf. 1670) 21
Henry Allen Conolly viii, ix, 82, 83, 86, 89, 90, 93, 101, 103, 104, 105, 106, 146
Henry Ernest viii, 82, 83
Henry (of Maddingly) 4, 39, 69, 77
Henry Herbert 128
Jane/Jeane (née Greenhill) 18, 21, 25
Jane (1662-1695/6) 22
Jane (1699-1766) 29
Jane (1739-1824) 32, 34
Jane (1823-1881) 57, 59, 69, 70, 73, 76, 78, 144, 147, 148, 149
Jane (b.1852) 78, 129
Joan Mary Woodham vii
Johan (wife of John Hurrell b.1575) 12

John (d. inf. 1669) 21
John (1575-1616) 8, 9, 10, 11, 12, 13, 15, 142
John Forbes 34
John Richard vii, viii
John Sopwith viii
Kate (b. 1859) 78
Lucy (née Gordon) 42, 55, 57, 58, 59, 63, 64, 65, 66, 67, 69, 73, 76, 77, 117, 118, 119, 125, 144
Lucy (b. 1814) 4, 57, 59, 65, 70, 73, 76, 77, 86, 144
Margaret (née Wale) 25, 27, 29
Margaret (dau of Allen Hurrell, d. 1746) 25
Maria Elizabeth 48, 49
Maria (1827-1876) 57, 58, 59, 67, 69, 70, 72, 76, 78, 79, 133, 144, 147, 148, 149
Marjorie 105
Martha (b. 1637) 17, 18, 22
Martha (née Sanxter) 39, 40, 42, 45, 48, 49, 145
Martha (née Perkins) 40
Mary (Maria) vii
Mary (1733-1748) 32
Mary (b. 1642) 17
Mary (b. 1744, née Hurrell) 34
Mary (b. 1807) 47, 48, 49
Mary (1829-1844) 57, 58, 59, 63, 65, 66
Mary (née Bailey) 57, 58, 70, 78, 125, 128, 129
Mary (Pollie) 3, 81, 82, 83, 89, 93, 95, 134
Mary Ann 34
Molly Elizabeth (1902-1994) ix, 104, 106, 107
Morris/Morrise/Morrice 9, 10, 12, 114
Phyllis vii, viii, ix, 3, 105
Priscilla (b.1570, "sister Puckle") 8, 11, 12, 15
Rachell (b. 1577, née Hurrell) 8, 9, 10, 11, 112, 114
Rebecca (née Pottrell) 40, 45, 53, 54, 70, 143
Rhodes (b. 1897) 105
Sara/Sarah (1648-1675) 16, 17, 18
Sarah (b. 1685) 21, 22, 138
Sarah (b. 1746) 34
Sarah (d. 1762) 13
Smith of Newton 34
Stewart 105
Susan(nah) (b. 1627) 17
Susan (b. 1667) 138
Susan(nah) (b. c1690) 28, 29
Swan of Newton 34
Swann (1781-1834) 40, 42, 48
Swann ('Iron Duke' b. 1816) viii, 4, 13, 40, 101, 114
Tamary Elizabeth (née Pritchard) 34
Theodosia (née Cavendish) 47, 48
Thomas (1565-1613) 8, 10, 11, 13, 15, 17, 50, 143
Thomas (1775-1815) 40, 42, 142
Thomasin (b. 1568) 8, 10, 11
William (b. 1604/05) 10
William (1645-1711) 17

Index of People

William (1696-1762) 27, 29, 31, 34
William (1736-1791) 3, 32, 34, 37, 38, 39, 42, 43, 67
William (c1800-1856) 47, 48, 49
William (1821-1878) 42, 48, 57, 58, 59, 65, 67, 68, 70, 71, 72, 73, 76, 77, 81, 82, 83, 86, 87, 93, 94, 103, 117, 134, 145, 147, 148, 149
William (b.1855) 78
William (Major 1857-1937) vii, viii, ix, 3, 5, 38, 39, 40, 42, 48, 49, 51, 54, 55, 56, 57, 58, 73, 77, 81, 87, 88, 89, 90, 91, 93, 94, 95, 96, 97, 98, 100, 101, 104, 105, 106, 107, 117, 146
William (b. 1882) 125
William Bailey (b. 1861) x, 78, 125, 127, 128
William Stacey (1766-1836) vii, 39, 40, 42, 43, 45, 46, 47, 48, 49, 50, 57, 58, 143
William (of Newton, 1673-1757) 22, 31, 138,139
William (of Newton, c1702-1779) 31, 22, 34, 43, 143
William (of Newton, d. 1830) 22, 34, 43
William (of Newton, d. 1854) 22, 34, 69
William (of Newton, d. 1902) 3, 4, 22, 34, 58, 65, 66, 67, 68, 69, 70, 72, 73, 75, 76, 77, 147, 148, 149
Iron Duke
    See Swann Hurrell
Jon
    Allen 22, 139
    Erasmus 22
    Jane (née Hurrell) 22, 139
    John 22, 139
    Joseph 22, 139
    Robert 22, 139
King
    Daniel 39
Knight
    Richard 28
    Susan(nah) (née Hurrell) 28
Kritzinger
    Ann (née de Clancy Walsh) vii, viii
Leroy
    Monsieur 69
Lilly
    Henry 17
    Susan(nah) (née Hurrell) 17
Loveday
    Jane 53
Major, The
    see Hurrell: **William** (Major 1857-1937)
Mackherry
    Mary 81
Martindale
    Ann (née Hurrell b.1797) 40, 46
    Charles 40, 42
    Charles William 40, 46, 47
    Elizabeth (née Hurrell b. 1770) 40, 42

Elizabeth (b. c1836) 49
Mayer
    Gladys Marion Millicent (née George) 133
    Sylvain 133
McGill
    Elizabeth (b.1889, née Hurrell) 128
    Hilton John 128
    Sandra 128
Metcalfe
    Edmund 47, 49
    Mary (b.1807, née Hurrell) 47, 49
    (Rev) William 49
Mortimer
    Jane (née Hurrell) 32, 34
    John Hamilton 32, 34, 143
Mouncey
    James Powell 120, 121
Musgrave
    Lady 47
Nash
    Arthur 49
    Maria Elizabeth (née Hurrell) 5, 48, 49
Nicholls
    G. 86
Ostler
    George 93, 104
Perkins
    Martha 40
Parker
    Rowland (author of *The Common Stream*) viii, 11, 18, 19, 38, 43, 45
Pottrell
    Jane (née Loveday) 53
    John 53, 143
    Rebecca 40, 45, 53, 54, 143
Prater
    Frances 70
    Henry 70
Price
    Rice 31
    Ann (née Hurrell) 31, 34
Pritchard
    Hannah (née Vaughan) 34
    John Forbes 34
    Mary Ann 34
    Tamary Elizabeth 34
Puckle/Puckell
    William (16th C) 8
Puckle/Puckell cont.
    Priscilla (née Hurrell) 8, 11, 12, 15
Rawlins
    Susan ix

Index of People

Regan
    Agnes 128
Rhodes
    Cecil 100
Rider
    Charles 58, 66, 72, 73, 75, , 76, 92, 147, 148, 149
Roundell Palmer
    Mr (Chancery Court) 75
Roupell
    Mr (Chancery Court) 75
Sanxter
    Martha 39, 40, 42, 45, 48, 49
Scott
    Harriet 86
Seekamp
    Ellen 66
Seddon
    Jane (née Hurrell) 28
    John 28
Singleton
    Nathaniel 16, 18, 31
    Sarah (b. 1648, née Hurrell) 16, 18
Smith
    Ann 31, 34
    Elizabeth Matilda 125
    George 12
    Mr (Chancery Court) 75
Smyth
    Henry Kennedy (Harry) M.B. 95, 134
    Mary/Pollie (née Hurrell) 95, 134
Snellock
    Alice 16
    Edward 16
    Robert 16
Spark
    Margaret 27
Spoomes
    Dorothie (née Hurrell) 12
Stacey
    Ann 32, 37, 39, 42
    Thomas (of Trumpington) 43
    William (of Newton) 43
Stanton
    Charles 82
    Mary Florence 82
    Maria (née Head) 82, 83
Stebbing
    John 108
Stone
    Edith Charlotte 103, **104**, 105, 106
    Elizabeth 104
    Erasmus 104

Stuart
    Hilda 5
Swann
    Robert 22
    Elizabeth 22, 31
Taylor
    Mr. 66, 67, 68
    John Debede 72, 147
Thurgood
    Mr. 59
    Elizabeth 9, 10, 12, 15, 16, 17
Toplis
    Edward 149
    Henry John Fuller 57, 59, 65, 66, 67, 68, 70, 76, 77, 86, 117, 147, 148, 149
    James 57, 67, 70, 147, 148, 149
    Lucy (b. 1814, née Hurrell) 20, 55, 59, 63, 65, 68, 73, 76, 77, 80, 86, 146, 147, 148, 149
(Unknown surname)
    Mary Ann 122
Vaughan
    Hannah 34
Wale
    Gregory 27
    Margaret (née Spark) 27
    Margaret 27, 29
Walsh/de Clancy Walsh
    Ann vii, viii
    Doreen (née Bell) ix, x
    John ix, x
    Philippa vii, viii, 4
    Phyllis (née Hurrell) vii, viii, 3, 105
Warburton
    Henry (Rev) 13
Warren
    (Sir) Richard 37
Wayte (vars. Wait/Waite/White)
    Elizabeth viii, ix, 81, 82, 83, 86, 87, 89, 93, 95, 98, 103, 144
    Emma 83, 144
    Hannah 82, 83
    Honour/Honor 82, 83
    Mary (b. 1832) 83
    Mary Agnes (b. 1833) 83
    Sarah 82, 83
    William 82
Webb
    Anna 22, 27, 31, 120
"West"
    Maria (see also Cranmer/Gordon) 121
Welbore
    John 31

Index of People

Williams
    Amelia Matilda 128
    Lieutenant 96
Winton
    (Mr.) James 118, 120
    Mrs (see also Greygoose) 118
Wood
    Col. 96
Wright
    Ann 70

Index of Hurrells/Hurrills of Sible Hedingham and their spouses, whose relationship to the main Hurrell line in this book has yet to be established.

Chandler
    Ann (née Hurrell) 113
Hurrell
    Agnes (dau. of Wm of Warners) 111
    Agnes (dau. of John (d. 1596)) 113
    Alice (b.c1573) 111
    Allse (m. Thomas Hurrell) 111
    Amy 111
    Ann (b. c1586 dau. of Morrice) 112
    Ann (dau. of John (d. 1635)) 113
    Augustine/Austin (b. c1577 s. of Morrice) 112
    Christopher (s. of Wm of Warners) 111, 112
    Christopher (b. c1577) 111
    Edward (s. of John (d. 1596)) 113
    Elizabeth 113
    George (d. c1706) 110
    Giles 114
    Hannah (d. 1807) 13
    Henry (b. c1583, s. of Morrice) 112
    Jeane (m. Christopher Hurrell) 112
    Jeane (dau. of John (d. 1598)) 113
    Joane (b.1569) 111
    Joane (b.1580) 113
    Joane (dau. of Wm of Lamarsh) 112
    John (b.1588) 114
    John (of Bloyes) 110
    John (of Hurrontes) 110, 111
    John (d.1596) 113
    John (d.1598) 113
    John (d.1635) 113
    John (s. of John (d. 1598)) 113
    John (s. of John (d. 1635)) 113
    John (s. of Wm of Warners) 8, 111, 113
    John (senior) 110
    John (of Warners) 8, 110
    Jonathan 115
    Katheryn 113
    Margaret (dau. of John (d. 1625)) 113
    Margaret (m. Roger Hurrell) 8, 109
    Margaret (dau. of Roger Hurrell) 8, 109
    Margh (b. 1572) 113
    Mary (m. John Hurrell (d.1635)) 113
    Mary (b. c1583 dau. of Morrice) 112
    Maud (dau. of Roger Hurrell) 8, 109
    Morrice (s. of Wm of Warners) 111, 112
    Morris (b. c1580 s. of Morrice) 112
    Moses (b. c1602 s. of Morris) 112
    Nicholas (s. of Wm of Warners) 111, 112
    Nicholas (s. of Wm of Lamarsh) 112
    Parnell (dau. of John (d. 1596)) 113
    Rachell (b. 1593) 114
    Rachell (b. 1594) 114
    Rachell (d. 1639) 114
    Richard 111
    Robert 111
    Roger (d. 1540) 8, 109, 142
    Rose (b. 1590) 114
    Susan (b. 1563/4) 113
    Susan 114, 115
    Susan (née Masson) 115
    Thomas (senior) 110
    Thomas (16th C) 110
    Thomas (17th C) 114, 115
    Thomas (s. of John (d. 1635)) 113
    Thomas (s. of Wm of Warners) 110
    Thomas (b. c1563) 113
    Thomas (b. c1588) 111
    Thomas (d. 1616) 111
    Ursley (b. 1580) 114
    Urslie 114
    William (d. 1562) 13
    William (s. of John (d. 1635)) 113
    William (senior) 110
    William (of Lamarsh, d. 1612) 8, 111, 112, 113
    William (of Warners) 8, 110, 111, 112, 113
    William (s. of John (d. 1596)) 113
    William (s. of John (d. 1598)) 113
    William (s. of John (d. 1635)) 113
    William (son of Roger Hurrell) 8, 109
    William (b.1563) 113
    William (b.c1585) 111
    William (of Warners) 8, 113
    William (s. of Wm of Lamarsh) 112
Hurrill
    George 113, 114
    Jane (née Curry) 114
    Nicholas (of Castle Hedingham) 114
    Thomas 113, 114
Levitt
    Margaret (née Hurrell) 113

BV - #0183 - 230326 - C41 - 234/185/11 - PB - 9781908223326 - Gloss Lamination